Annotated Edition

One Faith, One Lord
REVISED AND EXPANDED

A Study of Basic Catholic Belief

Gloria Hutchinson
Moya Gullage, S.H.C.J.
Dr. Norman F. Josaitis
Rev. Michael J. Lanning, O.F.M.
Jane P. Keegan, R.D.C.

Special Consultant
Rev. Msgr. John F. Barry

Official Theological Consultant
Rev. Edward K. Braxton, Ph.D., S.T.D.

William H. Sadlier, Inc.
9 Pine Street
New York, NY 10005–1002

Nihil Obstat
Reverend James J. Uppena
Censor Deputatus

Imprimatur
✠ Most Reverend George O. Wirz
Diocesan Administrator
Auxiliary Bishop of Madison
June 7, 1993

The *Nihil Obstat* and *Imprimatur*
are official declarations that
the work contains nothing
contrary to Faith and Morals.
It is not implied thereby that
those granting the *Nihil Obstat*
and *Imprimatur* agree with the
contents, statements, or
opinions expressed.

Home Office:
9 Pine Street
New York, NY 10005-1002

ISBN: 0-8215-2198-5
    456789/9876

Acknowledgments
Excerpts from *Good News* Bible,
copyright © American Bible
Society 1966, 1971, 1976

CONTENTS

Part One — Before You Use *One Faith, One Lord*

Part Two — Session Overviews

Part Three — Student Text with Annotations

Overview of the Program

Foundations of Catholic Belief

One Faith, One Lord, as a study in basic Catholic belief, recognizes what has taken place within the Catholic Church. That is why the text's main thrust is to help young people rediscover the solid foundation of Catholic belief. One Faith, One Lord senses the urgency among Catholic educators and catechists to "pass on" the truths Catholics continue to hold sacred. In spite of all the change, certain unalterable truths still remain firm as the bedrock of our faith. Our faith is strong because it is founded on the eternal word of God and God's promise to be with the Church always.

One Faith, One Lord helps catechists pass on to young people the fundamental doctrines of the faith in clear and concise language appropriate to the age level. The text adheres faithfully to the truths proclaimed by the Church down through the ages. Through this study young people can recognize and take pride in their Catholic heritage and tradition. Furthermore, they can come to a deeper understanding of what it means to be a Catholic—the recognition that being a Catholic is a gift, a privilege, and a responsibility. To be a Catholic means to be committed to continuing the mission of Jesus Christ in this world.

Experience/Reflection

The opening pages of each chapter of One Faith, One Lord approach the study of the beliefs of our Catholic faith by examining some basic human questions young people have about life. These questions, valuable in themselves, provide young people with a way of looking at and understanding realities that both permeate and transcend the human situation—experiences of the divine, of God.

The dynamics of life experience lead to an appreciation and development of faith. The source book of this faith is God and God's word in the Scriptures and in the teaching and Tradition of the Church.

Faith Development

Three key points of Catholic doctrines are clearly and concisely developed and summarized. Throughout One Faith, One Lord, the young people are led to understand the interrelatedness of the divine and human in their lives. The young people are drawn from recognizing their own life questions to an understanding of basic Catholic belief, to an integration of both in their personal lives. The word of God in Scripture is integrated throughout each chapter.

Faith Response/Decision

The integration of life experience and faith development leads naturally to a response in faith. This response is expressed first in the ability to reflect on and summarize the faith content of the session. This in turn leads to practical expression of that faith in action, and finally to prayerful reflection and celebration.

One Faith, One Lord presents the young people with the roots of a unified faith and belief in one Lord—the one faith that gives support and life to those who believe and trust in his words: "I came that they might have life and have it to the full" (John 10:10).

Components of the Program

The One Faith, One Lord program comprises three books: the student's text, the teacher's annotated edition, and the journal for the young person.

Text

Written in simple, straightforward style, the text focuses on the presentation of Catholic teaching in a format that addresses the interests, questions, and concerns of young people. In the sixteen chapters, the young people explore their Catholic faith and are helped to integrate their faith into their lives. The text also serves as a review of essential beliefs of the Catholic Church.

Annotated Edition

This book is a combination of an annotated student's text and a guide for the teacher/catechist. The annotated text contains a brief overview of the chapter, points to be stressed, and discussion questions. Certain sentences are underlined in red to highlight key ideas in each chapter.

The Guide provides complete and detailed information pertinent to teaching the **One Faith, One Lord** program either as a semester course or a full-year program. Its principal features are the following:

- *A Faith Assessment Session Preview* is provided for use before the program begins. This one-page inventory can be duplicated in the style of a blackline master. The preview offers an opportunity for the catechist/teacher to explore *with* the young people the dimensions of their faith and for catechists/teachers to find ways to nourish that faith. Care should be taken to underscore that faith is a gift from God. We cannot give faith to anyone, but we can help faith to grow.

- *Session Plans* are provided for teaching each of the sixteen chapters in the students' texts. Charts show how the sessions can be taught in alternative ways with varying time frames—five days, three days, or once a week.

- *A Postscript Session,* to be used at the end of the program, offers opportunities for the catechist/teacher and the young people to evaluate their learning experience.

- *Prayer* opportunities are given in each chapter for the group to praise God and celebrate their faith.

- *Action* sections in each chapter provide the young people with the opportunity to reflect on and make specific decisions to put their faith into action.

- *A Liturgical Year* section provides the young people with a clear and valuable reference to the seasons and feasts of the Church's liturgical year.

- *For Better Understanding* explains key points of our faith and guidelines for reading the Bible.

- *Glossary* of terms provides a handy reference to help the young people familiarize themselves with the meaning of terms and expressions used in the text and integral to Catholic teaching.

Teaching the Program

One Faith, One Lord can easily be adapted to a variety of learning-teaching situations. It is vitally important, however, that catechists/teachers be in dialogue with the Director of Religious Education and/or principal well before using these materials. Some determination must be made about the following:

- Will One Faith, One Lord be used over one academic year, a semester, a quarter, or in a summer program?
- What are the specific learning needs of the young people in your group this year? Which young people will need more time and extra help?
- What is the best way of adapting One Faith, One Lord to meet the specific needs of *your* group?

Experienced catechists/teachers know that they must adapt and tailor any catechetical resource to suit specific goals and needs. How else can they construct and organize toward any learning goal? It is the responsibility of catechists/teachers to use judiciously the time allotted to them for each session. This assures that the planned material will be covered adequately and completely. The learning-teaching process can only be enhanced by careful coordination of planning, selection, and timing.

The sixteen basic chapters in this Guide correspond to the sixteen chapters in the One Faith, One Lord text. Each chapter in the Guide offers *Adult Background* for the catechist and a *Session Plan* for teaching the corresponding chapter in the text.

Adult Background

This material is designed to help the catechists identify in a personal way the Christian message they wish to communicate. It provides a full yet simple presentation of the teaching and tradition of the Church that underlies the key issues of the lesson to be taught. It offers catechists an opportunity to:

1. acquire necessary background information and enrichment about the content of the particular chapter;
2. internalize the subject matter through a process of personal application to one's own life and experience. At various times opportunities are given to meditate or reflect on a given Scripture passage. It is highly recommended that the catechists use the space provided on these pages to record their responses to the questions and meditations, not unlike the journaling experience many often have as part of their spiritual life.

This preparation and process of internalization of the chapter material will not only benefit and enrich the spiritual life of the catechists/teachers, but also prepare them to share with young people on a deeper and more personal level the struggle, the searching, and the richness of their own faith commitment.

Three charts are offered to show how each session might be treated in alternative ways according to a five-day, a three-day, or a once-a-week program.

Session Plan

This part of the *Session Plan* begins with questions about a life experience relevant to young people. The teaching strategy is that by opening with a life experience, the young people will come to recognize that all life has a religious dimension. This opening experience always ends with questions to draw the young people into the two major parts of the *Session Plan* to be further developed and enhanced.

Five-Day Program				
Opener	Point 1	Point 2	Point 3	Review
Experience/ Reflection	*Faith Development*	*Faith Development*	*Faith Development*	*Faith Response/ Decision Prayer*

Three-Day Program		
Experience/Reflection Point 1 *Faith Development*	Point 2 *Faith Development*	Point 3 *Faith Development* *Faith Response/Decision Prayer*

Once-A-Week Program			
Given the time constraints of a once-a-week program, the results from the *Faith Assessment Survey* will determine what key doctrinal points need most emphasis.			
1. Engage young people in examining their own questions about life and faith: *Experience and Reflection*	2. Discuss: *Faith Development*	3. Summarize key teachings: *Faith Development*	4. Pray and plan to act: *Faith Response/Decision*

Faith Development

This part of the *Session Plan* leads the young people to study, reflect on, and endeavor to understand the three key doctrinal teachings of the Church developed in this particular session. It is accomplished by:

● presenting in a lively and interesting way the story of the faith;

● introducing the important Scripture passages that complement the doctrinal teachings;

● being introduced to complementary background about the Church in the "Do You Know . . ." feature.

Faith Response/Decision

The concluding part of the *Session Plan* offers the young people an opportunity to make personal and communal response to what has been experienced, understood, and appreciated through *Things to Think About* and *Things to Share*.

Young people are encouraged to take home their personal journals and their **One Faith, One Lord** Journals. Reading over and reflecting on the contents of these two books will add clarity to what they are learning about their faith and help them to understand their own questions more clearly. Moving from reflection to prayer will help them arrive at practical decisions as to how to express their faith in action.

 # Learning Techniques

Catechist Presentation

The adult teacher presents the material in such a way as to help the young people recognize and articulate their own perceptions and ideas while inviting them to accept freely and thoughtfully the beliefs and values of the Christian community.

Peer Presentation

One, two, or more group members, with the assistance of the catechist, presents a topic with which the total group is concerned. The presentation should include ways in which all can react and respond.

Group Discussion

Good group discussion blends both spontaneity and structure. The catechist can help the group to focus on a topic, to respect the contributions of each member, to make sure that all group members have a chance to speak, and to conclude when the discussion has run its course. All should be encouraged, but not forced, to participate.

Personal Prayer

One Faith, One Lord recognizes how important it is to help young people develop both skill and ease at personal prayer. The text and guide offer suggestions complementary to each chapter. Learning also takes place when we worship together and when we serve one another and the wider community of which we form a part.

Personal Journal

Many young people are already familiar with keeping a diary. Encouraging them to record in a journal their thoughts, questions, and reflections on their experiences is teaching them an important means of self-reflection and growth. Journals are recommended as a way of helping the young people internalize the concepts and experiences shared. The Journal for **One Faith, One Lord** is especially designed to do this.

Roleplaying

This technique offers young people the opportunity to "walk in someone else's shoes" and to "see things through someone else's eyes" as they take on character roles and briefly act out a situation which they may or may not have personally experienced. Through the technique of roleplaying, young people can observe how they and others respond and develop skills that will assist them in everyday life.

Brainstorming

Brainstorming is a way to elicit as many ideas and solutions as possible on a particular topic or problem. No idea or solution should be subject to criticism or negative comment. After the ideas and suggestions have been listed on newsprint or a chalkboard, everyone reflects on the list. This is followed by a guided discussion.

Guest Speakers

Some topics might be enhanced by input from an outside source. We can help young people to grow as persons of faith by structuring opportunities for them to meet, hear, and converse with Catholics whose faith positive values are central to their personal and professional lives.

Scripture Reflection

One Faith, One Lord offers many appropriate passages from the Scriptures for reflection and discussion. The catechist can assist young people to benefit from such reflection by explaining the context and meaning of a given passage, by creating an environment conducive to such reflection, by making sure that the passage is read with preparation and care, and by stimulating discussion on the passage once it has been read and reflected upon.

Using Visuals

The visuals and accompanying captions in the text can serve as visual statements of the content, as links to activities in the *Session Plan,* or as catalysts initiating joy, wonder, or excitement.

Different people see different things in the same photo. For this reason, a good visual can provoke an interesting discussion. Here is a simple formula for discussing a photo. Ask:
● What do you think is happening in the picture?
● How do you think the people in the picture feel?
● How does this picture make you feel?
● Why do you think this picture is included in this chapter?

Using Audiovisuals

Videos, films, and audio cassette music tapes are found to be effective tools for communicating religious truths. In planning for a session:
● check first with your own parish media library to see what is available;
● review the resources available from your diocesan media center;
● do not overlook resources available from neighboring parishes/schools and your local library;
● order all materials well in advance; **PREVIEW, PREVIEW, PREVIEW** all materials before the planned showing date. You will avoid disasters in this way!

Here is a list of producers and/or distributors from whom audiovisual materials can be ordered:

Center for Media & Values
1962 S. Shenandoah Street
Los Angeles, CA 90034

Don Bosco Multimedia
475 North Avenue P.O. Box T
New Rochelle, NY 10802

First Run/Icarus Films
153 Waverly Place
New York, NY 10014

St. Anthony Messenger and Franciscan Communications
1615 Republic Street
Cincinnati, OH 45210

GIA Publications, Inc.
7404 S. Mason Avenue
Chicago, IL 60638

Ikonographics
P.O. Box 801
Croton-On-Hudson, NY 10520

Learning Corporation of America
1350 Avenue of the Americas
New York, NY 10019

Liturgy Training Publications
1800 N. Hermitage Avenue
Chicago, IL 60622-1101

Maryknoll World Productions
Maryknoll, NY 10545

Mass Media Video Ministries
2116 N. Charles Street
Baltimore, MD 21218

The Media Guild
11722 Sorrento Valley Road
San Diego, CA 92121

Pyramid Film and Video
P.O. Box 1048
Santa Monica, CA 90406

Brown-ROA
2460 Kerper Blvd.
P.O. Box 539
Dubuque, IA 52004

North American Liturgy Resources
10802 North 23rd Avenue
Phoenix, AZ 85029

Weston Priory Productions
Weston, VT 05161

Preview Session

This session will help the catechist/teacher and the young people to explore what they already believe, value, and question about their faith.

1. Provide each person with a copy of the *Faith Assessment Inventory.* Ask the young people to write "I wonder" statements about each of the categories listed on the Inventory. After they have finished, provide time for those who wish to share their responses with the whole group. (You may wish to save the young people's responses as a point of reference for the *Postscript Session.*)

2. Using a similar list, ask the young people to circle one of the numbers 3, 2, 1, or 0 after each of the statements. By circling a number, they will indicate how important that particular belief is in their life now. Use the following as a scale: 3—very important in my life; 2—somewhat important in my life; 1—not very important in my life; 0—not sure. After the young people have indicated their responses, invite those who wish to discuss their reactions in small groups.

3. Tell the young people that the last part of the *Inventory* will help them to measure their progress as they journey through their study of faith together.

4. Now have the young people turn to the *Table of Contents* in their textbooks. Point out the similarity between the list of topics to be covered and the list of items on the *Faith Assessment Inventory.* Let them page through the rest of the book. Then ask for a general reaction to the book and answer any questions they may have.

5. Invite the young people to reflect quietly for a few minutes, while you play some quiet background music. Ask them to pray for themselves and one another as they begin this program and search for God and truth together.

6. Conclude by asking them to reflect for a few minutes and then answer the following statement in their journals: **I have questions about. . .**

Faith Assessment Inventory

A. You are invited to write "I Wonder" statements about each of the categories listed below.

When I Think of . . .   I Wonder . . .

a) God _____

b) the origin of the world _____

c) evil _____

d) Jesus Christ _____

e) the Holy Spirit _____

f) Mary _____

g) the resurrection _____

h) the Church _____

i) the Commandments _____

j) death _____

k) the sacraments _____

l) sin _____

m) helping others _____

n) prayer _____

o) peace and justice _____

p) life _____

q) love _____

B. Circle the number that expresses how important each of the following beliefs is in *your* life:
3—very important in my life; 2— somewhat important; 1—not very important; 0—not sure.

What I Believe About . . .

a) God .... 3................... 2................... 1................... 0

b) the origin of the world .... 3................... 2................... 1................... 0

c) evil .... 3................... 2................... 1................... 0

d) Jesus Christ .... 3................... 2................... 1................... 0

e) Mary .... 3................... 2................... 1................... 0

f) the resurrection .... 3................... 2................... 1................... 0

g) the Church .... 3................... 2................... 1................... 0

h) the Holy Spirit .... 3................... 2................... 1................... 0

i) the sacraments .... 3................... 2................... 1................... 0

j) the Commandments .... 3................... 2................... 1................... 0

k) the Eucharist .... 3................... 2................... 1................... 0

l) heaven .... 3................... 2................... 1................... 0

m) helping others .... 3................... 2................... 1................... 0

n) prayer .... 3................... 2................... 1................... 0

Postscript Session

This session will help the catechist/teacher and the young people evaluate what they have learned, measure their progress in knowledge and understanding, and consider some directions to take in living as a Catholic.

1. Have the young people look at the "I wonder" statements they had written in the *Preview Session*. Ask them to draw up another list and consider whether or not their original questions have been answered and if any new ones have been added as a result of this program.

2. Using a similar list, ask the young people to circle one of the numbers 3, 2, 1, or 0 after each of the faith statements. By circling a number, they will indicate how important that particular belief is in their life now. Use the following as a scale: 3—very important in my life; 2—somewhat important in my life; 1—not very important in my life; 0—not sure.

3. Form groups of five and give each group a large sheet of newsprint and felt-tipped markers. Their task is to write a group essay on the topic: *What Does It Mean to Be a Catholic?* If the group wants to illustrate their essay with pictures and symbols, encourage them to do so.

4. Concluding with a prayerful reflection would be appropriate, giving thanks for the growth that has taken place within each of the young people during this program and asking God's Spirit to direct them in the future, to enable them to live what they have learned, and to help them grow in their relationship with God.

5. Allow time for the young people to complete the following statement and record it in their journals: **Something I have learned this year that has made my faith stronger is. . .**

   Invite those who wish to share their insights aloud.

Faith Assessment Inventory

A. You are invited to write "I Wonder" statements about each of the categories listed below.

When I Think of . . .   I Still Wonder . . .

a) God _____

b) the origin of the world _____

c) evil _____

d) Jesus Christ _____

e) the Holy Spirit _____

f) Mary _____

g) the resurrection _____

h) the Church _____

i) the Commandments _____

j) death _____

k) the sacraments _____

l) sin _____

m) helping others _____

n) prayer _____

o) peace and justice _____

p) life _____

q) love _____

B. Circle the number that expresses how important each of the following beliefs in your life *now* after participating in this program: 3—very important in my life; 2—somewhat important; 1—not very important; 0—not sure.

What I Believe About . . .

	3	2	1	0
a) God	3	2	1	0
b) the origin of the world	3	2	1	0
c) evil	3	2	1	0
d) Jesus Christ	3	2	1	0
e) Mary	3	2	1	0
f) the resurrection	3	2	1	0
g) the Church	3	2	1	0
h) the Holy Spirit	3	2	1	0
i) the sacraments	3	2	1	0
j) the Commandments	3	2	1	0
k) the Eucharist	3	2	1	0
l) heaven	3	2	1	0
m) helping others	3	2	1	0
n) prayer	3	2	1	0

Enjoying the Good Bread of Prayer

Who of us would want to face a demanding task on an empty stomach?

"A loaf of bread," the Walrus said,

"Is what we chiefly need. . . ."

(Lewis Carroll)

Prayer is the loaf of bread we need to nourish us for the challenging ministry of catechesis. Without it, we falter like malnourished marathoners who fail to reach the finish line.

In recent years Catholics have rediscovered the joy of praying with God's word and listening as God speaks to us in the Scriptures. Study groups and prayer groups have formed, and people are reaping the benefits of modern biblical scholarship in new and ever more satisfying ways. How exciting that Scripture has become an integral part of most varieties/methods of prayer. Below are six of these varieties of "wholesome bread." They can be eaten alone or shared.

Praying the Hours

For those who enjoy structured scriptural prayer, the Liturgy of the Hours offers ample seasonal fare. Many Catholics anchor their day with Morning Prayer from this ancient prayer of the Church and settle themselves in God's presence at sundown with Evening Prayer.

Following a pattern of psalms, readings from Scripture and great Christian writers, and intercessions, the Hours link us with the universal prayer of the Church. They frame our day in prayerfulness, enabling us to say with Saint Augustine, "Let no day go by in which I do not bless Thee."

Praying Creation

Nature's pantry is overflowing with enticements to prayer. All we need is alert senses and an appetite for praise. Praying with God's gift of creation costs only a little time. As Annie Dillard advises, "*Spend* the afternoon. You can't take it with you."

Nourish yourself with the bread of prayerful attention to sunrise and stars. . . walking mindfully through gardens or woods. . . attending to birdsongs and water music. . . hiking leisurely among hills or strolling along beaches. . . appreciating squirrels in the park or lions in the zoo.

Whether we live in a city or in a rural community, nature is around us. Even in a busy office we can experience nature: a beautiful plant on the desk, a shaft of sunlight streaming through the window. Praying in this way with regard to the world around us reminds us of our responsibility to care for God's creation, too.

Praying with Saints

As athletes have trainers, we have the saints to advise us in seeking the bread of prayer. Choose one or two saints (preferably one of each sex) who seem best suited to serve as your personal prayer trainers. First and foremost we have Mary, the Mother of God, who remembered all the things that God had done for her and who "thought deeply about them" (Luke 2:19).

Look for books, articles, or videos in which your chosen saints' ways of prayer are described. Adapt their ways to your own situation.

Praying with an Icon

The word *icon* means "image." Icons are beautiful religious images that "speak more to inner than to our outer senses. They speak to the heart that searches for God," writes Henri Nouwen in *Behold the Beauty of the Lord: Praying With Icons*. For example, we all know what it feels like when someone we love is absent, and we are pining to see him or her. Out comes the favorite photograph. In beholding the image, we nourish the relationship.

The process can hold true in our friendship with Jesus. With an icon of Jesus, He who appeared to be absent becomes present. We are better able to "behold him, consider him, contemplate him and desire to imitate him" (Saint Clare of Assisi).

Choose an icon that draws you. It might be Christus Pantokrator (Christ, Ruler of the Universe) or Christ the Teacher. Light a candle or burn incense before it. Fasten your gaze on the Holy Face in patient and loving attention.

Praying Your Journal

When the Lord wanted the Israelites to know how they would be freed from slavery, God instructed Jeremiah to "write down in a book everything that I have told you" (30:2).

Keeping a spiritual journal is a way of following this divine advice. We desire to be freed from the slavery of false images of God and ourselves. By recording our dreams and doubts, inspirations and intuitions, causes of joy and sorrow, conversions and failures to be open to a change of heart—the ups and downs and blessings of daily living—we can see God's handwriting in our daily lives.

Jesus insists that the Kingdom of God is within us. A journal helps us discern how God's Kingdom is either breaking through or being blocked within us. It clarifies our personal story of salvation, revealing how we are co-authors with God of this unique narration.

Praying by "Doing Nothing"

The hearty bread of contemplative prayer requires no reading, writing, walking, or talking. It is, in fact, so simple that we may find it "impossible." For to be a true contemplative, one must be able to focus one's life completely on the Lord's presence. In the depth of one's heart, one waits for and listens to the Lord.

When a novice asked the Trappist monk Thomas Merton how to pray, the master responded, "How does an apple ripen? It just sits in the sun."

When Martha got all steamed up about Mary's failure to lend a hand in the kitchen, Jesus reminded her that "one thing is needful"—just sitting at His feet and being present to Him. The centering prayer invites us to "be still and see that I am God."

To experiment with the prayer, sit with your back straight, breathe deeply, and move into your inner temple. Choose a simple prayer word. Repeat it silently within yourself to "launch into the deep."

Then let go of the word and sit in the Lord's presence. Do nothing. Use the prayer word only to deter distractions. After a few minutes, close your prayer time by saying a favorite prayer.

From these six good loaves, select the ones that seem best suited to your spiritual appetite. "Whatever the way that leads you most frequently to the awareness of God," says Meister Eckhart, "follow that way." And remember the advice of other spiritual writers to try different forms of prayer as you seek a well-balanced spiritual life. Our Church tradition treasures many forms and many styles of praising and thanking God.

Lord, Teach Us to Pray

We all need to be taught how to pray. One of Jesus' disciples asked Him, "Lord teach us to pray." So might we all ask.

As a catechist, you are in a privileged situation to lead young people in prayer and to provide them with good experiences of prayer. Your own personal efforts to learn how to pray and to develop a prayerful attitude will help you communicate the importance of prayer in life.

Through an openness to and a preparation for prayer, your everyday experiences can take on deeper meaning and become contact points for personal prayer. The above background and practical suggestions provide only a beginning. The rest is up to you. Like the great saints and mystics, we learn to pray by praying.

1 Our Catholic Roots

Goal: To appreciate the sources of our Catholic faith

Adult Background

When you say that you know a person well, you indicate that you have had more than an occasional encounter with that person. You have done more than observe his or her activities and accomplishments; you have talked to the person, read his or her diary, or corresponded in some way. In other words, the person has "revealed" his or her inner self to you.

Left to ourselves, we could know something of God from creation, for the world around us is a blueprint of the Creator. And our reason tells us that the Creator must be wise and intelligent. But just as people must reveal their inner selves to us in order for us to know them well, so must God reveal the divine Self to us in a special encounter.

That is the reason we say that revelation is God telling us about God's own Self. It involves the saving actions of God in our history. Revelation takes place in the living experience of people in a community of faith. It is an interpersonal communication between God and people within the history of a community.

God's wonderful and special act of revelation began with the Chosen People, the Israelites, and continued with Jesus and the apostolic community. When it came time to write about their unique experience of God, the prophets and the apostolic community expressed themselves in the testimonies of faith we have come to call the Old and New Testaments. The Bible, or Scripture, therefore, is not itself revelation. It is the written record of God's revelation in the faith community.

Preparing the Session

Read through the entire session and familiarize yourself with the annotations provided, as well as materials needed, if any. *Determine what your specific learning objectives are for this session.* Adapt the following plans according to your gifts, the needs of your young people, and the time period provided.

It may be helpful to plan the number of minutes you wish to give each section of the lesson. There are spaces provided below for this purpose. Doing this will insure that you will cover *completely* the material for the session.

Now, look at all the photographs and illustrations in this session. Choose those that you want to highlight as integral and most appropriate to your specific lesson plan. Be sure to preview any audio-visuals you may have selected.

Experience/Reflection (_____min.)

1. Young people are familiar with TV talk shows. Ask them to suggest a different format for a program called QUEST, which would deal with questions about life. Have them read the first paragraph on text page 5. Allow time to write out their questions and share them in groups of three.

2. Ask whether the young people have seen any adventure movies. Have them think of the images of explorer and quest as they read the second paragraph. Then have them write out their imagined answers. Lead a brainstorming session to elicit their "answers to all of life's questions."

3. Have them read the last four paragraphs, stressing the importance of life's questions.

Faith Development (_____min.)

4. Have the young people read section one on page 6 and follow with a discussion

on the different ways people find answers to questions.
- Where do you turn for answers to our questions?
- Which way have you found most helpful? Give examples

Talk about the limitations of human experience. Stress that faith, a gift from God, brings a whole new way of looking at life. Faith helps us to see things from a different point of view.

5. Share answers to the two concluding questions. Tell the young people to ask a parent or an adult the same two questions and then compare answers.

6. Have them interview the same adult (or another of their choice) on how they came to know God.

7. Tell the young people to read section two on page 7, relating it to their own experience. Ask questions such as these:
- When you were a child, did anyone ever tell you that thunder and lightning were signs that God was angry?
- Have you ever looked up at the universe and the stars and felt that there must be a God?
- Where do you find God now? List responses to the last question on the chalkboard or on newsprint.

8. In groups of three, have the young people describe the results of their adult interviews, which were talked about above. Then ask:
- What did you learn in your interview?
- What impressed you most in your interview?
- How did the adult answers compare with yours?

Share together how all human beings search for God, and prepare the young people for a discussion of the concept of revelation.

9. The Church uses the word *revelation* in a special way to describe God telling us about God's own Self. Point out that although God reveals who God is in many ways—in creation, in human events, and in people—God also revealed who God is in a special way to the Israelites and to the apostolic community. Review some of the truths God has made

known to us that are listed on page 7. Highlight also the response we make to God's revelation through personal and communal prayer.

10. Ask the young people to recall family stories that are typically repeated at family gatherings. Discuss why families do this. Then have the young people read section three on page 8. Review how and why the Bible came about from the spoken word, or oral tradition, to the written word under God's guidance, or inspiration.

11. Ask what type of books they like to read (short stories, history, poetry, etc.). Review the different types of writing in the Bible. Ask: How and why are the two main parts of the Bible different?

    Summarize by asking, "How would you explain to someone who wants to be a Catholic what the Bible is and why it is such a holy book for us?"

12. Review the meaning of the word "tradition" in *Do You Know* and complete the *Words to Remember.* Use the *Church Teachings* for a deeper understanding of the whole session. Highlight that revelation is not merely a set of statements.

Faith Response/Decision (_____min.)

13. Introduce the concept of journaling as a way to pray. Begin with a hymn to establish a prayerful, quiet atmosphere and pray aloud that God will guide the young people this year. Suggest that they begin their personal prayer journals by reflecting on the two questions in *Things to Think About* and by writing down their thoughts and decisions.

14. Allow time for them to reflect on the question in *Things to Share* and exchange their answers with a partner.

15. For further prayerful reflection, encourage the young people to use pages 6–7 of the *One Faith, One Lord* Journal.

2 God the Creator

Goal: To appreciate the true wonder of God's creation

Adult Background

The opening words of the Bible are "In the beginning, when God created the universe...." With these words the biblical story of creation begins. Read the poetic account in Genesis 1:1—2:4, noting the repetition of key words and phrases such as "then God commanded," "let there be," "God was pleased," "evening passed and morning came."

If the young people hold a literal view of the creation story, that is, that God created the world in six actual days, point out the second creation narrative (Genesis 2:5–23), which describes the order of creation differently. Which account is correct? The answer, of course, is both. Without books, people learned by listening. Therefore, the "six-days" and the repeated phrases were literary devices used to teach religious truth. Each author was expressing religious truth in a way that people could understand and remember. The author of Genesis did not intend to be scientific in the story of creation. In the picturesque language of poetry, the author wanted to convey the truth that God created everything that exists. Before anything else came to be, God was!

A literal interpretation, therefore, robs the Genesis story of its true impact. As the Second Vatican Council observed: "Those who search out the intention of the sacred writers must, among other things, have regard for `literary forms.' For truth is proposed and expressed in a variety of ways, depending on whether a text is history of one kind or another, or whether its form is that of prophecy, poetry, or some other type of speech. The interpreter must investigate what meaning the sacred writer intended to express and actually expressed in particular circumstances as he used contemporary literary forms, in accordance with the situation of his own time and culture. For the correct understanding of what the sacred author wanted to assert, due attention must be paid to the customary and characteristic styles of perceiving, speaking, and narrating which prevailed at the time of the sacred writer."
Dogmatic Constitution on Revelation, 12

Preparing the Session

Read through the entire session and familiarize yourself with the annotations provided, as well as materials needed, if any. *Determine what your specific learning objectives are for this session.* Adapt the following plans according to your gifts, the needs of your young people, and the time period provided.

It may be helpful to plan the number of minutes you wish to give each section of the lesson. There are spaces provided below for this purpose. Doing this will insure that you will cover completely the material for the session.

Now, look at all the photographs and illustrations in this session. Choose those that you want to highlight as integral and most appropriate to your specific lesson plan. Be sure to preview any audio-visuals you may have selected.

Experience/Reflection (_____min.)

1. Have the young people read the first four paragraphs on text page 11 and then imagine the scenario. Invite reactions.
2. After they read the fifth paragraph, allow time for them to reflect on the questions and to write their answers in the space provided. Invite responses.

Faith Development (_____min.)

3. Suggest that the young people underline the answers to the following questions as they read section one:

- What book of the Bible tells us about God and the creation of the world?
- Did the author of Genesis give us a scientific explanation of how the world was created?
- Why did the author describe God as creating the world in six days?
- What religious truths are being expressed in the creation story?

Allow time for reading and answering the questions, then invite responses.

4. Before having the young people read aloud the creation stories in Genesis, remind them that the author of Genesis is trying to teach us the great truth that God created the world. The Genesis account is not a scientific explanation of how the world came to be. Then invite those assigned to read aloud the creation account.

5. Review the section *How to Find Your Way in the Bible* and make sure that the young people can distinguish among books, chapters, and verses in the Bible. You might want to refer them to *Helps to Understanding the Bible* on page 115.

6. Have the young people read section two on page 13 and underline in their books the answers to these questions:
- What does the Genesis account tell us about the creation of human life? (We alone are created in the "image and likeness of God.")
- How do human beings differ from other living beings in God's creation? (No other creature can think, choose, and love in the likeness of the Creator.)
- How can human beings grow in God's image? (To grow in God's image, we must use our minds, make responsible choices, and open our hearts to love.)

7. Play quiet background music as you open the Bible, which has been set up in a special place in the room. Slowly and reverently read aloud Psalm 8. End the reading by saying, "The word of the Lord," and have the group respond, "Thanks be to God."

8. Have the young people read silently Psalm 8 on text page 13. As they read, have them consider the question "How are we special in God's creation?" and underline phrases that help them to

answer this question.

9. Emphasize that creativity, an inner sense of self-worth, goodness, etc. must be present in us if we are made in God's image and likeness. Ask them to think about these qualities and then write a response in their journals to the concluding question on page 13.

10. Ask: What is our responsibility towards creation? Tell the group to use this question as a focal point as they read section three on page 14.

11. Stress the notion of creation as ongoing and our responsibility to develop and use our talents and abilities. In groups of three, have the young people discuss what people their age might do in their home, school, neighborhood, or parish to care for and improve the environment.

12. Ask them to reflect on the concluding question and personalize their answer as an essay, a poem, or a collage.

Faith Response/Decision (_____ min.)

13. Have the young people take turns slowly reading aloud *Church Teachings About Creation* as you play instrumental music. Invite an exchange of ideas about why scientific theory can be compatible with Catholic belief.

14. Have the young people define the terms in the *Words to Remember* section.

15. Ask the young people to reflect on the two questions in *Things to Think About*.

16. In pairs, have them share answers to the two questions in *Things to Share*. Pray the concluding prayer together.

17. For further prayerful reflection, encourage the young people to use pages 8–9 of the *One Faith, One Lord* Journal.

# 3 The Fall and the Promise

Goal: To understand the origin of evil

Adult Background

No one escapes tragedy in life. In the face of tragedy—whether big or small—we look for reasons; we seek explanations; we ask, why me?

In this chapter the young people begin to probe a particular tragic situation through the story of Erica. Take time to read page 17 to better understand what the young people are experiencing.

From your own experiences and those of your friends, recall individuals who faced tragedy and overcame it through personal resources and with the help of others. Present these examples to help the young people to see that life is both tragic and beautiful.

The acceptance of tragedy as a part of the human condition still does not answer the deeper questions. How did suffering enter into a world created good by God? Was there an original goodness and happiness that human beings once had with God, but which was somehow lost?

Carefully read Genesis 3:1–23. Note how the author describes the first man and woman as breaking their friendship with God and shattering their own happy existence.

In approaching the topic of original sin, it is important to clarify the fact that we are born into a sinful condition, yet we are not personally responsible for this condition. We live in a sinful world. We find within ourselves the tendency and inclination toward evil. In our personal lives, we make choices either to give in to the pull towards evil, thereby committing personal sin, or choose to respond to the good through the grace of God.

The Genesis story does not end in tragedy; it ends with the promise of salvation. Genesis 3:15 can be understood as the first promise of a redeemer: the Messiah, or Savior, who would come to save God's people.

Preparing the Session

Read through the entire session and familiarize yourself with the annotations provided, as well as materials needed, if any. *Determine what your specific learning objectives are for this session.* Adapt the following plans according to your gifts, the needs of your young people, and the time period provided.

It may be helpful to plan the number of minutes you wish to give each section of the lesson. There are spaces provided below for this purpose. Doing this will insure that you will cover *completely* the material for the session.

Now, look at all the photographs and illustrations in this session. Choose those that you want to highlight as integral and most appropriate to your specific lesson plan. Be sure to preview any audio-visuals you may have selected.

Experience/Reflection

1. Choose two volunteers to roleplay a scene in which some of Erica's friends visit her in the hospital before or after her new beginning. Ask the players to make the dialogue express the tragedy and the hope of the situation. After the scene, write "Hopeless situation?" on the board. Invite responses and discuss the roleplay. Ask: What is the tragedy and the hope of Erica's situation?

2. As a follow-up activity, allow time for the young people to reflect on the final questions on page 17 and share responses in groups of three.

Faith Development (_____min.)

3. Begin by sharing personal stories of tragedy and hope. Then ask the young people to read section one on page 18, keeping the following questions in mind:

- How did the author of Genesis try to answer the question "Why is life both beautiful and tragic?"
- According to the Genesis story, how did sin and evil enter the world?
- What was the cause of this break in the relationship between God and the first man and woman?

4. Ask for volunteers to dramatize the Genesis story on page 18. Then ask the young people to respond to the question at the end of this section.

5. Have the young people read section two on page 19 and make a chart of the symbols used in the Genesis story and their meaning. Stress that the meaning of each symbol helps us to understand a religious truth, that is, a truth that will help us to live in relationship with God. Call attention to the gift of grace, a sharing in the life and love of God.

6. Review the process from temptation to sin outlined on the top of page 20. Discuss how hard it is sometimes to resist doing the wrong thing, especially when it seems good for us.

7. Invite the young people to imagine how they might react to the following situation:

    A friend invites you to a party next Friday night and wants an answer to the invitation right away. You know all your friends will be there. You also know there will be drinking at the party. What would you decide to do?

    Suggest that they write in their journals what they would do in this situation and the reasons for their decision.

    After a time for reflection, ask volunteers to read their responses. Discuss the priorities involved in making difficult decisions. Review the meaning of original sin and its effects.

8. Ask the young people to read silently section three that begins on page 20. Have them recall the promise God made to the first man and woman: that God would send a Savior. Have them discover what kind of Savior, or Messiah, would come to restore God's people.

    After reading the section, discuss:
    - When God's people were discouraged and without hope, who spoke for God to encourage them? (The prophets reminded the people that God had not forgotten them.)
    - What kind of Messiah was described by the prophets? (The Messiah would restore the people's relationship with God.)
    - What did Jesus, the "New Adam," do for us? (He restored us to God's life and love.)
    - At Mass, what great mystery of faith do we proclaim? (Through Jesus' life, death, and resurrection, He saves us from evil and shares God's life and love in a human way.)

9. Review the description of the suffering servant in the *Do You Know* section on page 20. Have someone read aloud the scriptural quotation from Isaiah. Then use the *Church Teachings* on page 19 for a deeper understanding of the whole session.

10. Have the young people define the terms "original sin," "grace," and "garden" in *Words to Remember*.

Faith Response/Decision (_____min.)

11. Ask the young people to recall all that they have learned in this session as they pray the acclamation that we often use at Mass. Then suggest that they respond in their journals to the two reflection questions.

12. Ask the young people to reflect on the two questions in *Things to Think About* and express their answers in a poster, a collage, a poem, or an essay. Then in pairs have them share responses to the question in *Things to Share*. One person can act as a non-believer, while the other explains the meaning of the Genesis symbols.

13. For further prayerful reflection, encourage the young people to use pages 10–11 of the *One Faith, One Lord* Journal.

4 Jesus, the Promise Fulfilled

Goal: To appreciate Jesus and His message

Adult Background

Even in Israel's darkest hour when the people were led into exile in a foreign land, God was with them, reminding them of the promise God had made to send a Savior.

In the prologue to his Gospel, John proclaims the unexpected way God's promise to send a Savior was fulfilled and how the Promised One was received: "He came to his own country, but his own people did not receive him. Some, however, did receive him and believed in him; so he gave them the right to become God's children" (John 1:11–12).

The Incarnation, or the mystery of the Son of God becoming Man, is the basis of our hope that we can become more like God. In choosing Mary to be the Mother of God and preserving her from sin, God shows us that the human person can be made holy.

In the early Church, various controversies centered on the question of who Jesus was. That same question remains with us today. Young people need help to formulate, clarify, and deepen their faith in Jesus as the Son of God. You may want to write in your own words what we believe as Catholics about Jesus Christ. This personal statement of your beliefs will help you share more deeply with the young people your own faith in the Incarnation.

The Blessed Trinity was not revealed to test our faith or confuse our belief. Rather, it was revealed to tell us something about God and, therefore, something about ourselves in relation to God. Briefly, the doctrine of the Trinity means that while God is one, God is not solitary. God is community—God the Father, who is the originator and creator of life, sends the Son for our salvation and communicates the Spirit for our rebirth in water and the Spirit.

The revelation of God as Father, Son, and Holy Spirit tells us first of all what God is to us. But even more important than knowing *about* God is knowing God.

Preparing the Session

Read through the entire session and familiarize yourself with the annotations provided, as well as materials needed, if any. *Determine what your specific learning objectives are for this session.* Adapt the following plans according to your gifts, the needs of your young people, and the time period provided.

It may be helpful to plan the number of minutes you wish to give each section of the lesson. There are spaces provided below for this purpose. Doing this will insure that you will cover *completely* the material for the session.

Now, look at all the photographs and illustrations in this session. Choose those that you want to highlight as integral and most appropriate to your specific lesson plan. Be sure to preview any audio-visuals you may have selected.

Experience/Reflection (_____min.)

1. Have the young people read text page 23 and then list their ideas about the possible contents of the wallet. Invite comments on what the contents might tell us about the owner.

2. Have them list the items in their own wallets (or knapsacks, purses, or pockets). In groups of three, have them share what these items might tell others about them. Make the point that to gain insight about someone who is not physically present, we must rely on clues, like the contents of the wallet or observed and recorded behaviors. Point out that the people of Israel were looking for clues about the One whom God had promised to send.

Faith Development (_____min.)

3. Have the young people read the first two paragraphs of section one on page 24 and underline the clues by which the prophets pointed to the promised Savior. (He would be in the family of David, born in Bethlehem, a great leader, the Messiah.) Review these with the young people, elaborating on the meaning of the term "Messiah."

4. Have them read the two gospel selections about Jesus' coming on page 24. Highlight the amazement of Mary and Joseph at how unexpectedly God would fulfill the promise through them. Mary was troubled. Joseph was torn by doubt. Yet both of them placed their trust in God's word and promise.
    After reading the rest of page 24, ask the young people to reflect on the following questions and invite them to respond in their journals:
    *   Have you ever felt that God has entered your life in an unexpected way?
    *   Do you accept God even in persons you find difficult to get along with?
    *   Why do you think Mary and Joseph responded as they did to God's message? Would you have responded in the same way?

5. Recall the wallet story and ask, "Where do we get our knowledge of Jesus?" Then have the young people read section two on pages 25–26. Elaborate on the meaning of the word "Incarnation"—the Second Person of the Blessed Trinity becoming one of us. Stress that this is a central truth of our Catholic faith.

6. Have the young people answer the two questions at the end of this section and discuss their answers.

7. Recall that throughout their long history, God's people experienced God's presence and identity through many different signs. Ask the group whether they can remember any of these signs (the burning bush, manna, the ark of the covenant, the Temple).
    Have the young people read section three on page 26. Then discuss:
    *   The identity of God is revealed in Jesus.

What does Jesus tell us about God?
*   What can we learn about God from Jesus' words and actions?

8. Talk about the Kingdom of God. Have the young people look for images of the Kingdom of God given in the parables. In groups of three, have them discuss what each one can do to help bring about God's Kingdom of justice, peace, and love in their home, school, and neighborhood. Then have them describe the Kingdom of God in their own words and write it in their journals.

9. Review in the *Do You Know* section how we express our relationship to the Trinity at Mass. Then ask the young people to take turns slowly reading aloud the truths presented in *Church Teachings* on page 25 as you play quiet music.
    Assign *Words to Remember* for home study.

Faith Response/Decision (_____min.)

10. Slowly pray the Glory to the Father together, giving thanks to God for the gift of Jesus our Savior. Then ask the young people to read slowly the Second Vatican Council's description of the Incarnation given in *Things to Think About*. Invite them to record their thoughts in their journals.

11. Play quiet music and lead the group through a reflective meditation. Have them choose a setting, such as a mountain, lake, wheat field, or village, and picture themselves there as one of Jesus' followers listening to Him talk about the Kingdom. Have them record their thoughts about Jesus and His teachings about the Kingdom of God.

12. For further prayerful reflection, encourage the young people to use pages 12–13 of the *One Faith, One Lord* Journal.

5 Jesus the Savior

Goal: To understand Jesus' passion, death, and resurrection

Adult Background

To some of the people, Jesus was the Messiah for whom they had waited. He held them spellbound with the message that the Kingdom of God was theirs. When Jesus spoke to the crowds in a way that no one else had done, He did not spare them from the harsh truth that following Him would entail suffering. These stark words did not sit well with the crowd, or even with Jesus' closest followers. Yet the idea that the Messiah would have to suffer was hinted at by the prophets.

Jesus did not live up to some people's messianic expectations. Instead, He chose to follow the single purpose of His mission: to do the will of His Father. Because Jesus' mission ran counter to these expectations, it meant inevitable rejection, possibly death. Outright rejection of Jesus came quickly on the heels of His triumphant entry into Jerusalem. Jesus' crucifixion and death confirmed the belief of many that Jesus could not have been the Messiah. But those who experienced the risen Christ believed in His victory over death. The forces of sin and evil did not have the final word.

Suffering is not an end in itself. We need hope so as not to be overwhelmed by our present sufferings. For Christians, the basis of hope is our faith in the power of Jesus' resurrection and His promise that we will rise with Him. As Saint Paul said, "If Christ has not been raised from death, then we have nothing to preach and you have nothing to believe.... If our hope in Christ is good for this life only and no more, then we deserve more pity than anyone else in all the world" (1 Corinthians 15:14, 19).

Perhaps your personal reflections on these words will help you to share more deeply with the young people the meaning of Jesus' mission.

Preparing the Session

Read through the entire session and familiarize yourself with the annotations provided, as well as materials needed, if any. *Determine what your specific learning objectives are for this session.* Adapt the following plans according to your gifts, the needs of your young people, and the time period provided.

It may be helpful to plan the number of minutes you wish to give each section of the lesson. There are spaces provided below for this purpose. Doing this will insure that you will cover *completely* the material for the session.

Now, look at all the photographs and illustrations in this session. Choose those that you want to highlight as integral and most appropriate to your specific lesson plan. Be sure to preview any audio-visuals you may have selected.

Experience/Reflection (_____min.)

1. Have the young people look at the picture on pages 28–29 and direct their attention to the two questions on page 28. Then ask them to read the short sketch about Joseph Lister on page 29. Invite volunteers to tell in their own words how Lister showed purpose and vision in spite of difficulties and obstacles.

2. Have the young people answer the questions on page 29 and write their answers in the spaces provided. Invite a sharing of responses, then ask:
   - What impressed you most about this scientist? (Answers will vary.)
   - What gave meaning to his life? (The opportunity to better the lives of people gave meaning to his life.)

Faith Development (_____min.)

3. Pose the following questions:
   - Was Jesus a crowd pleaser?
   - Did Jesus allow others to control Him?
   To help the young people answer these questions, have them do a Gospel search of episodes in which Jesus seems to be acting contrary to the crowd or, in some cases, contrary to those in authority:
   Matthew 9:1–8   Luke 4:14–30
   Mark 14:60–64   John 6:1–15
4. Have the young people read section one on page 30. Tell them to underline or refer to specific parts of what they read in order to answer these questions:
   - How did Jesus avoid being controlled by the crowd? (Jesus, at times, fled. At other times, He refused to be the kind of Messiah the crowd expected.)
   - What kind of Messiah did most of the crowd expect? (They looked for a political king who would help them overthrow the Romans.)
5. Have them answer the concluding question on page 30. Invite responses.
6. Ask the young people to read section two on page 31. Help them deepen their understanding of what they have read.
7. Ask for some volunteers to roleplay the following situation: You are one of Jesus' disciples. Jesus has just been crucified. You try to explain your feelings at this moment to some friends who did not know Jesus.
   Discuss the roleplay and then ask the young people to write their reactions in their journals. Invite volunteers to read their reactions to the rest of the group.
8. Direct their attention to the question at the end of the section. Allow time for them to reflect on it and invite their responses.
9. Write the following words on the board or newsprint: life, pain, ridicule, rejection, and death. Ask the group to suggest any feelings that these words bring to mind.
10. Ask the young people to read section three on page 32. Have them compare their feelings with those of the original disciples. Stress how the resurrection of Jesus changed the disciples from fearful persons into courageous persons capable of spreading the message of Jesus. Explain that it gave them a new vision of life, pain, suffering, ridicule, rejection, even death, and that it can do the same for us today when we place our faith in the risen Lord.

11. Ask the young people to recall experiences of ridicule and rejection in their own lives. Ask how Jesus' response in the face of ridicule and rejection can make a difference in the way they can now face such experiences. Conclude with a reflection on Jesus' resurrection.
    Begin to prepare the young people to understand that we celebrate Christ's saving death and resurrection all during the liturgical year. You may wish to refer them to pages 117–119 in their texts, pointing out the centrality of the Easter Triduum.
12. Ask volunteers to read aloud *Church Teachings*. Have the entire group respond by saying the prayer together. Then have them do the *Words to Remember* section.

Faith Response/Decision (_____min.)

13. Point out that in Baptism God calls us to share in Jesus' triumph over death. Have the young people consider that we must "die to selfishness and sin" in order to be raised to become the "good news." Ask them to name one special thing they can do this week to become Jesus' good news of love, justice, and peace to someone else.
14. Ask the young people to reflect on the two questions in *Things to Think About*. Then in pairs, have them share answers to the two questions in *Things to Share*.
15. For further prayerful reflection, encourage the young people to use pages 14–15 of the *One Faith, One Lord* Journal.

# 6 Jesus Sends the Holy Spirit

Goal: To appreciate the Spirit's role in our lives

Adult Background

At the end of His public ministry, Jesus promised to send the Spirit to His disciples. However, Jesus also told His disciples that it was only through His suffering and death that they would receive the Spirit.

One way the world can know that Jesus' death was not the end is that the Spirit is still alive in His followers. This dynamic concept runs throughout the New Testament. The central theme of this session is that today, two thousand years after Jesus' death and resurrection, the Holy Spirit is still present and active in the Church.

Read prayerfully the passage from Acts 2:1–4 concerning the first Pentecost, as found on page 39. Underline words or phrases that refer to the action of the Spirit. After Pentecost, the apostles remained the same people they always had been. But now, through the active presence of the Holy Spirit, they had the strength and courage to carry out the mission they had been given by Jesus.

As with the apostles long ago, the Spirit calls each one of us here and now, urging us toward a more complete union with God and others. Because God's Spirit brings "love, joy, peace, patience, kindness, goodness, faithfulness, humility, and self-control" (Galatians 5:22–23), to be a Christian means to be identified by these characteristics.

The Holy Spirit is the source of all activity in the Church. The Holy Spirit unites the members into one living body with Christ as Head, allowing each person to grow according to his or her gifts. "There are different kinds of spiritual gifts, but the same Spirit . . . The Spirit's presence is shown in some way in each person for the good of all" (1 Corinthians 12:4,7).

Reflect for a moment on the presence of the Holy Spirit in your life and in the lives of people around you. Think, too, of how the Spirit has guided our Church in renewal since the Second Vatican Council. Where will the Church be 100 years from now? What will it look like? Certainly we cannot tell today. But we can say with confident assurance that the Holy Spirit will be with us to guide us to that new age. This is Christ's promise to us.

Preparing the Session

Read through the entire session and familiarize yourself with the annotations provided, as well as materials needed, if any. *Determine what your specific learning objectives are for this session.* Adapt the following plans according to your gifts, the needs of your young people, and the time period provided.

It may be helpful to plan the number of minutes you wish to give each section of the lesson. There are spaces provided below for this purpose. Doing this will insure that you will cover *completely* the material for the session.

Now, look at all the photographs and illustrations in this session. Choose those that you want to highlight as integral and most appropriate to your specific lesson plan. Be sure to preview any audio-visuals you may have selected.

Experience/Reflection (_____min.)

1. Direct the young people's attention to the two questions on page 36. Then have them read page 37 and ask them:
   ● If people such as Rachel Carson do not speak out and act, what might happen to our environment?
   ● What are some other areas in which we can perceive the Spirit acting through individuals and groups to preserve and renew life?
   ● What can cause a group, a team, a community to lose its "spirit?"

2. Have the young people answer the two questions that conclude this section and share their responses in groups of three.

Faith Development (_____min.)

3. Invite the young people to read section one on page 38. Then ask:
   - If a group lacks spirit, goals, or vision, what may happen to it?
   - How did Jesus insure that His followers would have vision and "spirit"? (Jesus asked His Father to send the Holy Spirit.)
   - What did Jesus say the Spirit would do for them? (Jesus said the Spirit would remain with them and in them; teach them and help them remember Jesus' words; lead them to the truth; and give them strength.)

4. In advance, prepare task cards with a scriptural reference on each one. Give each person a task card. Allow time for them to look up the passages and report on what each one tells about the role of the Holy Spirit. Use these passages:
   Romans 8:1–4   Galatians 3:1–5
   Ephesians 3:14–21   1 Timothy 4:1–7
   1 Peter 1:10–12   1 John 5:5–12

5. Ask the young people to read and underline the various meanings of the word "Paraclete" in *Do You Know*.

6. After the young people read section two on page 39, have someone read aloud the description of the coming of the Spirit (Acts 2:1–4). Then ask:
   - How were the apostles different after the Holy Spirit had come to them?
   - How did the Holy Spirit both comfort and challenge the apostles?
   - After receiving the Holy Spirit, what were the apostles prompted to do?
   - What is the Good News that the apostles preached?

7. Briefly, have the young people elaborate on ways in which fire is helpful to humanity. Ask why fire is an appropriate symbol of the Holy Spirit.

8. Stress that the early Christian community was extremely devoted to the practice of caring for one another, as we read in Acts 2:42–47. Have the young people reflect on the concluding question and share responses.

9. Ask the young people to think about a time when they were almost too afraid to do or try something. Make a list of these fears on poster board. Invite several young people to share their stories.

10. Invite volunteers to prepare a roleplaying situation showing how they would calm someone's fears in one of the situations described above.

11. Then ask the young people to read section three on page 40. Have them compare their feelings with those of the original disciples. Stress how the Holy Spirit changed the disciples from fearful persons into courageous persons capable of spreading the message of Jesus.

12. Ask the group to think about any fears they have in their lives right now. Conclude with a prayer to the Holy Spirit for strength, direction, and comfort. Use the two concluding questions as a review.

13. Together pray the prayer to the Holy Spirit on page 41. Then have them do the *Words to Remember*.

Faith Response/Decision (_____min.)

14. Ask the young people to reflect on the questions in *Things to Think About* and record their ideas in their prayer journals. Then, in pairs, have them share answers to the questions in *Things to Share*.

15. Ask volunteers to read aloud the key points in *Church Teachings* to review the theme and content of this chapter.

16. For further prayerful reflection, encourage the young people to use pages 16–17 of the *One Faith, One Lord* Journal.

7 The Catholic Church

Goal: To identify the Church founded by Christ

Adult Background

From among His followers, Jesus chose "the Twelve" to be the nucleus of the new community that would complete His mission. After Jesus' death and resurrection, they experienced the power of the Holy Spirit, and from that moment on they knew fully their mission was to preach Jesus to all persons. Belonging to Jesus' community was open to all who believed and were baptized in His name. It is from this one apostolic community, characterized by its universal call to holiness, that the Catholic Church grew.

When we say the Creed at the Sunday liturgy, we profess that "we believe in one, holy, catholic, and apostolic church." These are the marks of the Church. They describe realities of the Church's nature and identify its mission. As realities, they are gifts bestowed by the Lord, always present. As expressive of a mission, they are tasks and goals to be worked toward. In other words, these four marks of the Church are not merely doctrinal truths already possessed, but also dynamic challenges and ideals towards which we strive.

It is through striving together that we strengthen our bond of unity in the Lord—our witness to the world that Christ is present. Through His Spirit, Jesus is fashioning us, the Church, into His people.

Meditate on these words of Saint Paul in preparation for this session. "Do your best to preserve the unity which the Spirit gives by means of the peace that binds you together. There is one body and one Spirit, just as there is one hope to which God has called you. There is one Lord, one faith, one baptism; there is one God and Father of all mankind, who is Lord of all, works through all, and is in all" (Ephesians 4:3–6)

Preparing the Session

Read through the entire session and familiarize yourself with the annotations provided, as well as materials needed, if any. *Determine what your specific learning objectives are for this session.* Adapt the following plans according to your gifts, the needs of your young people, and the time period provided.

It may be helpful to plan the number of minutes you wish to give each section of the lesson. There are spaces provided below for this purpose. Doing this will insure that you will cover *completely* the material for the session.

Now, look at all the photographs and illustrations in this session. Choose those that you want to highlight as integral and most appropriate to your specific lesson plan. Be sure to preview any audio-visuals you may have selected.

Experience/Reflection (_____ min.)

1. Direct the young people's attention to the two questions on page 42. Then have them read page 43. Ask whether they would add any identifying qualities to the list. Invite responses from the whole group.
2. Next have them do a similar process of identifying qualities of the Catholic Church to someone their age who is not a member of the Church. Ask the young people to engage in the self-reflection process before they define the Church's I.D. qualities.

Faith Development (_____ min.)

3. Ask the young people to think of a time when they felt they belonged to a group or a time when they felt left out. After sharing stories. Ask:
   - Why do people need to belong?

- How do people feel when they are rejected? How do you feel when *you* are rejected?
- In what situations can you make others feel that they belong?

4. Stress that if we accept our Baptism as a sign of belonging to Jesus Christ and His Church, we are also called to live as Jesus did. Then have them read section one on text page 44.

5. Draw attention to the sentence on page 44: "He made everyone feel like somebody." Ask the young people to list and share ways in which they each can make others "feel like somebody."

6. Ask the young people to read the first three paragraphs of section two on page 45. Ask: Which is more important to the human person, the eye or the hand? Allow time for discussion. Help them to realize that neither is more important than the other, that the eye needs the hand, and vice versa. Ask:
- What does this idea tell us about the Church?
- What does it mean to say the Church is *one?*

7. Now have the young people finish reading section two, and ask:
- What does it mean to say that the Church is *holy?*
- What does living life to the full have to do with being holy?
- What is the role of the Holy Spirit in the Church?
  After they complete the reading of section two on page 45, have them draw images or symbols to reflect their responses to the concluding questions.

8. Have the young people read section three on page 46. Ask:
- What is the meaning of catholic as a mark of the Church?
- To whom did Jesus entrust His Church?
- What was the mission of the apostles?
- What does it mean to say that the Church is *apostolic?*

9. Put the following chart on the board or on newsprint:

one	holy	catholic	apostolic

Ask the young people to write their impressions of the Church in the columns in which they seem to belong. Question them further to clarify their thoughts about the Church:
- Which mark of the Church seems to be most evident today?
- What can we do to make the other marks become more evident?

10. Individually or in groups, have the young people think of practical and positive ways in which they can act to promote respect for others' religious beliefs.

11. Tell the group to read *Do You Know* on page 45. Discuss what it means to say that Jesus left no detailed blueprint as to how the Church should look. Then have different young people read aloud the *Church Teachings* to review the chapter.

Faith Response/Decision (_____min.)

12. Plan a prayer service to celebrate belonging to the Church community. On a table with the Bible and a candle, place the images and symbols drawn by the young people. Open with an appropriate hymn. Have the young people take turns praying the leader's part in the prayer on page 47. Conclude with a celebratory song or hymn.

13. Ask the young people to reflect on the question in *Things to Think About* and record their thoughts in their prayer journals. In pairs, have them share answers to the first question in *Things to Share*. The personal nature of the second question also calls for journal writing.

14. For further prayerful reflection, encourage the young people to use pages 18–19 of the *One Faith, One Lord* Journal.

8 The Seven Sacraments

Goal: To know the meaning of the seven sacraments

Adult Background

One of the most appealing requests in the New Testament comes from Greek pilgrims who have arrived in Jerusalem to celebrate the Passover. They go directly to Philip and say, "Sir, we want to see Jesus" (John 12:21).

Twenty centuries later our hearts still resonate with that request. We want to see Jesus and to be reassured that He remains with us always.

The Church responds to our request with seven grace-filled and effective signs. By these signs we are nourished, healed, and transformed as members of the faith community.

"What was visible in the Lord has passed over into the sacraments," observed Pope Leo the Great, suggesting why the sacraments are so vital in the lives of those who desire to see and follow Christ. What Jesus does and says in the Gospels we encounter Him doing in our lives.

Each sacrament marks a particular time of growth for us as Christians and invites us to share in God's grace in a special way. Through the three sacraments of initiation (Baptism, Confirmation, Eucharist), we become fully initiated members of the Church, charged with carrying out the mission of Jesus Christ in the world. The two sacraments of healing (Reconciliation and Anointing of the Sick) restore us when we experience a "brokenness" in our physical or spiritual lives. The two sacraments of service (Matrimony, Holy Orders) assist those who are called to the married state and those called to ordained ministry in the Church.

God has spoken to us most effectively through the sign language of the Word, who became flesh. Through the sign language of the sacraments, we grow ever deeper in our relationship with Christ and with each other.

We learn by our lives to speak the language of love.

Preparing the Session

Read through the entire session and familiarize yourself with the annotations provided, as well as materials needed, if any. *Determine what your specific learning objectives are for this session.* Adapt the following plans according to your gifts, the needs of your young people, and the time period provided.

It may be helpful to plan the number of minutes you wish to give each section of the lesson. There are spaces provided below for this purpose. Doing this will insure that you will cover *completely* the material for the session.

Now, look at all the photographs and illustrations in this session. Choose those that you want to highlight as integral and most appropriate to your specific lesson plan. Be sure to preview any audio-visuals you may have selected.

Experience/Reflection (_____min.)

1. Invite the young people to look at the pictures on pages 48–49. Then ask them to consider the questions on page 48.
2. In preparation for this session, introduce the group to Sr. Thea Bowman. After reading page 49, ask the young people to think about the three reflective questions. They need not respond publicly to the first question, but encourage an open discussion of the other two. Then give a brief overview of the three faith issues they will explore in this session.
3. Ask the young people to discuss the universal sign of friendship, the handclasp. Remind them that originally it was used to show that the open hand held no weapon. Discuss:
   • What does a handclasp signify?

Faith Development (_____ min.)

4. In preparation for section one on text page 50, help the young people to understand the great story of the exodus of the Israelites from Egypt and their coming to the Promised Land. You may wish to refer to the Old Testament Book of Exodus to refresh your memory about Moses, the Passover, etc. The story of the manna is in Exodus 16.

   Have the young people read section one. Then ask for responses to the following questions:
   - What attitude did God expect of the Israelites before sending them a sign that fulfilled their needs?
   - How did the Israelites interpret ordinary signs such as light, rain, and the like?
   - How is Jesus a sign of God's love?
   - Do you think God continues to communicate with us through signs?

   Challenge the young people to answer the final questions on page 50 and to do a Bible search in support of their responses.

5. Have a volunteer read section two on page 51 and discuss the questions at the end of the section. If time allows, encourage the young people to do research about those in the Church who carry out its mission of service. Display and discuss the information. You may wish to contact the service organizations of your own diocese, such as Catholic Charities, for more information.

   The *Do You Know* on page 51 concerns the gift of infallibility. Oftentimes people remark that the Church, which is to be a sign of God's life and love, can fail in seeking after justice and the furthering of God's Kingdom. We forget that the Church is also a human organization. The gift of infallibility, however, assures us of the integrity and truth of our basic beliefs. Remind the young people of this gift and of their responsibility to pray for the Church and its leaders.

6. Read section three on page 52. Ask:
   - In which sacraments do we share God's life of grace? (all of them)

- What do the sacraments invite us to do? (carry out Jesus' mission)
- How can you be a sign of God's love? (by caring, sharing, loving)

Explain the three groupings of the sacraments and the purpose for each grouping (initiation, healing, service). For a further explanation of the sacraments, refer to summary statements 11 and 12 on pages 113–114 of the text.

7. Use *Church Teachings* for a deeper understanding of the whole session, as well as for review.

Faith Response/Decision (_____ min.)

8. Allow time for the group to discuss *Things to Share* on page 53. Place special emphasis on the role of the community assembly in sacramental celebrations. If possible, invite a guest speaker to help the young people see how integral God's word is in each sacrament and how we are united with the Church community in these celebrations. Remind the group again that liturgy means our *public* worship. This is truly the "work of the people."

9. Create a mood of calm and quiet for prayer. Invite the young people to reflect on *Things to Think About*. Refer to the sacraments chart on page 116 in the *Faith Summary* section of the text. Help the young people to look briefly at each of the seven sacraments and note the columns "Signs We See" and "Signs We Hear." Engage the young people in a discussion of sacramental celebrations in which they have participated. After this, encourage them to make their journal entries.

   Conclude this time together with a few moments of quiet prayer and gather these together as one with the prayer on page 53.

10. For further prayerful reflection, encourage the young people to use pages 20–21 of the *One Faith, One Lord* Journal.

9 Becoming Catholic

Goal: To understand the process of Christian Initiation

Adult Background

Many who have chosen as adults to become members of the Catholic Church say they were drawn not only by doctrine or ritual but by a sense of belonging. They have come into the Church through the RCIA (Rite of Christian Initiation of Adults). And they have experienced the process of initiation as an affirming journey into a community of faith.

We who were baptized as infants and confirmed as children or young teens need the witness of these committed people. They help us to appreciate the Sacraments of Initiation as well as our own call to evangelize others by sharing our stories of how God has been present to us.

"We all catch the faith together," said one catechumen, referring to the conversion of the baptismal candidates and the renewed conversion of their sponsors within the order of Christian initiation.

They share an intensive experience that begins with hospitality or welcoming, continues through the "rite of acceptance" and "journey of faith," culminates in Baptism, Confirmation, and Eucharist at the Easter Vigil, and continues in the Easter season.

How should initiation into the Church, by whatever path, change us? Pope John Paul II writes, "It is of particular importance that all Christians be aware that through baptism they have received an extraordinary dignity" (*The Lay Faithful*, 1989). We are to become "active and responsible" partners in the re-evangelization that the modern world so clearly needs.

Anointed by the Holy Spirit as sons and daughters of the Most High, we are commissioned to "go, then, to all peoples everywhere and make them my disciples" (Matthew 28:19). If we fail to welcome others into the Church, we are missing the joy of "we all catch the faith together."

When we allow the grace of our Baptism and Confirmation to blossom progressively in us, others are drawn to the fire of God's life. As Cardinal Suenens observed, "A Christian is not fully a Christian unless he (or she) is a maker of Christians" (*Spiritual Journey*, 1990).

Preparing the Session

Read through the entire session and familiarize yourself with the annotations provided, as well as materials needed, if any. *Determine what your specific learning objectives are for this session.* Adapt the following plans according to your gifts, the needs of your young people, and the time period provided.

It may be helpful to plan the number of minutes you wish to give each section of the lesson. There are spaces provided below for this purpose. Doing this will insure that you will cover *completely* the material for the session.

Now, look at all the photographs and illustrations in this session. Choose those that you want to highlight as integral and most appropriate to your specific lesson plan. Be sure to preview any audio-visuals you may have selected.

Experience/Reflection (_____min.)

1. Write the word "welcome" on the board. Invite the young people to share any associations or memories they have with this word. Let them take the word apart and paraphrase it; for example:
   - You have *come—well* done!
   - Well, come!
2. Read pages 54–55 with the group. Invite anyone who may have been baptized recently to share his/her experience. Then ask for responses to the closing questions on page 55.

Faith Development (_____ min.)

3. Continue the discussion of being welcomed to ensure that the young people understand that the sacrament of Baptism includes a special way of welcoming us as members of the Church. Read section one on page 56.

   Have the young people examine the photographs on pages 56–57. Describe Baptism by immersion as shown on page 57. The person to be baptized, instead of having water poured over him/her, is immersed in water. This is how Baptism was celebrated in the early Church.

4. Discuss what it means "to welcome all without distinction . . . as Jesus did." If time allows, have the young people work in groups to research the following gospel stories:
   - Mark 12:41–44
   - Matthew 15:29–31
   - Mark 10:13–16
   - Luke 14:12–14
   - Mark 1:40–45
   - Luke 15:11–32

5. Discuss the concept of Christian Initiation. Then ask: What happens to us in Baptism?

6. Before reading section two, show the group a variety of pictures of water as cleansing, refreshing, powerful, life-giving, etc. Then read page 57.

7. Stress that *original* means "first." Original sin refers to the rejection of God's love by the first people. Baptism removes this sin from our lives and gives us a share in God's life, which we call *grace*. Encourage the young people to decide how they can best express their thanks for the gift of Baptism.

8. Have a volunteer read *Do You Know* on page 57. Stress that it is only in an emergency that anyone can baptize, but it is still the right of a baptized Christian to do this when necessary.

9. Now read section three on page 58 with the group. Discuss the connection between Baptism and Confirmation. Ask:
   - What does it mean to you to be "sealed with the Gift of the Holy Spirit"?
   - What are the gifts of the Holy Spirit? Ask the young people to reflect quietly before responding to the questions at the end of section three. Then suggest that they go over *Church Teachings* at home.

Faith Response/Decision (_____ min.)

10. As a prayerful response to this session, take the group, if possible, to your parish church. Explain to the group that making the sign of the cross with holy water is a reminder of Baptism.

    Invite the young people to sit quietly in God's presence and think about *Things to Share* on page 59. Then close by praying together the prayer on this page.

11. For further prayerful reflection, encourage the young people to use pages 22–23 of the *One Faith, One Lord* Journal.

10 The Eucharist

Goal: To value the sacrament of Christ's real presence

Adult Background

An African missionary was delighted to discover that the Masai word for Eucharist means "food for the heart." When we recall how Jesus celebrated the Eucharist with His friends at the Last Supper, we can appreciate how close to the mark the Masai word comes.

The Gospel accounts make it clear that Jesus fully intended and eagerly expected to provide His disciples with "food for the heart" before He was taken from them. He had made detailed preparations well in advance. And when the hour finally arrived, He told them, "I have wanted so much to eat this Passover meal with you before I suffer!" (Luke 22:15).

Jesus knows that the food He is about to offer will give life to the world. He knows that the giving will cost no less than His life. Yet as John's Gospel tells us, "He had always loved those in the world who were his own, and he loved them to the very end" (13:1).

Whenever we celebrate Eucharist worthily, we remember how Jesus invested Himself, Body and Blood, in providing us with this "food for the heart."

We remember "that we are more than we seem to be: that the Spirit of Jesus is constantly calling us to own up to who we are and reminds us of the great care that God has for all of us, especially for the poor and the oppressed" ("Liturgy Celebrates Life," Bishop Michael Pfeifer, OMI).

By this final sacrament of initiation, we are made one with Christ in communion and with Christ in the assembled community. We are reconciled, nourished, and sent to be the Body of Christ in the world.

Having prayed our Great Thanksgiving, we go forth to love and serve others who may have less cause to be grateful than we do. In some sense, our Eucharist is not complete until all authentic human needs have been satisfied. These include the needs of our children and youth for inspired religious teaching and spiritual guidance.

Preparing the Session

Read through the entire session and familiarize yourself with the annotations provided, as well as materials needed, if any. *Determine what your specific learning objectives are for this session.* Adapt the following plans according to your gifts, the needs of your young people, and the time period provided.

It may be helpful to plan the number of minutes you wish to give each section of the lesson. There are spaces provided below for this purpose. Doing this will insure that you will cover *completely* the material for the session.

Now, look at all the photographs and illustrations in this session. Choose those that you want to highlight as integral and most appropriate to your specific lesson plan. Be sure to preview any audio-visuals you may have selected.

Experience/Reflection (_____min.)

1. Take time to discuss the opening questions on page 64, allowing the young people to explore our human need to celebrate, remember, and even ritualize significant events.

   Talk about how human beings develop rites to celebrate significant events. We use special words, actions, and symbols. For example, think of the flag and fireworks on the Fourth of July. Challenge the young people to explain other "rituals" in their lives. Remind them how important ritual is, but also of the necessity of never losing sight of ritual's meaning and focus.

2. Have a volunteer read page 65 before asking for responses to the questions.

Faith Development (_____min.)

3. Read the first five paragraphs of section one. Have one of the group list on the board under the heading *Passover Meal* key words and phrases that describe this celebration (for example: sacrifice, blood, lamb, liberation, salvation). If time allows, have some young people do research and then roleplay a Passover meal for the rest of the group.

4. Finish reading section one with the paragraphs describing the Last Supper. Again, have someone list on the board under the heading *Last Supper* key words such as: sacrifice, blood, salvation, covenant. Then ask the group to add to the list what made this Passover with Jesus different from all others. (The sacrifice would not be a lamb but His Body and Blood.)

5. Explain that the word *Eucharist* means "thanksgiving." Ask: What do we give thanks for at Mass? Then discuss the closing paragraph concerning our remembrance of Jesus' saving death and resurrection, memorialized in the Eucharist.

6. Share with the group how the early Church first celebrated the Eucharist in people's homes. Only gradually, as the Church grew, did the ritual of the Eucharist take on a different style. However, the basic elements of the Eucharist have never changed throughout the ages: giving thanks to God in the assembly, proclaiming the word of God, remembering what Jesus did, and sharing in the breaking of bread.

   Have the group read section two. Ask the young people to compare the way the early Christians celebrated the Eucharist with the way we celebrate it today. Then use the closing questions to develop an awareness of how we are called to worship as Catholics. Write on the board or give the group copies of the times for parish weekend and daily Masses. If possible, plan to attend a weekend Mass together.

7. Use section three to develop an understanding of the Eucharist as both meal and sacrifice. Discuss the quote from the Second Vatican Council on page 68 before having the young people respond to the closing questions. Then ask the group to go over *Church Teachings* on page 69. Discuss the meaning of *transubstantiation*. This term is used to describe the sacramental mystery by which the bread and wine used at Mass become the Body and Blood of Christ. The bread and wine still *look* the same, but they are no longer really bread and wine. They have become the Body and Blood of Christ; they are now our spiritual food and drink. Jesus is with us under the appearances of bread and wine.

   Point out the *Do You Know* section on page 68. Explain the meaning of the eucharistic fast.

Faith Response/Reflection (_____min.)

8. Ask the young people to go over *Things to Think About* before the next session.

9. Gather the young people in a circle with their books. Create a quiet, peaceful environment. If possible, play instrumental music softly in the background. Invite them to do the meditation in *Things to Share,* imagining themselves at the Last Supper. After a few minutes, close with the prayer on page 69.

10. For further prayerful reflection, encourage the young people to use pages 24–25 of the *One Faith, One Lord* Journal.

11 The Mass

Goal: To understand our central act of worship

Adult Background

For many Catholics, the Mass remains a great feast at which they eat sparingly and participate reservedly in the "table conversation." As a Church, we are still moving toward the goal of restoring and promoting "full and active participation in the liturgy by all the people"*(Constitution on the Sacred Liturgy)*.

The Mass lies at the heart of who we are as Catholics. Even those who frequently "miss Mass" or settle for being passive observers recognize our common need to gather, admit our sinfulness, be reconciled, and stand together to praise and thank our God in whom we "live and move and have our being" (Acts 17:28).

How can we help one another and those we serve to experience the Mass as a vital, joyful, and prayerful celebration?

1) We can model and encourage active presence to one another as we gather for the liturgy. Be hospitable! Speak to, smile at, and welcome others at the family table.

2) We can model and encourage active listening to the word of God. Reflect on the readings at home before setting off for church. Listen with the attitude of a hungry guest who is being offered a variety of good foods. "Heed me, and you shall eat well, you shall delight in rich fare," says the prophet (Isaiah 55:2).

3) We can model and encourage active involvement in the Eucharistic Prayer by remembering what God has done in our lives, summoning a desire to give thanks, gathering the needs of those around us into our prayer, and making our responses with energetic conviction.

Finally, the most effective way to be full and active participants is to live our Amens. By our actions between liturgies we say Amen to justice, Amen to compassion, Amen to the peace of Christ.

Saint Augustine reminds us, "You cease to praise God only when you swerve from justice and from what is pleasing to God" ("Discourse on the Psalms").

Preparing the Session

Read through the entire session and familiarize yourself with the annotations provided, as well as materials needed, if any. *Determine what your specific learning objectives are for this session.* Adapt the following plans according to your gifts, the needs of your young people, and the time period provided.

It may be helpful to plan the number of minutes you wish to give each section of the lesson. There are spaces provided below for this purpose. Doing this will insure that you will cover *completely* the material for the session.

Now, look at all the photographs and illustrations in this session. Choose those that you want to highlight as integral and most appropriate to your specific lesson plan. Be sure to preview any audio-visuals you may have selected.

Experience/Reflection (_____min.)

1. Ask the young people whether they think of being able to go to Mass as a *gift*. Point out that sometimes we recognize the value of something only when it is gone. Tell the young people about places in the world where the celebration of the Mass is either discouraged for a variety of reasons or infrequently celebrated because of a lack of priests. People in such situations have been known to risk their lives or to walk for miles under terrible conditions to be able to participate in the Mass with others.

2. Point out the questions on page 70. After a period of discussion, ask volunteers to

read page 71 and respond to the final questions. You may wish to invite your parish priest, a visiting missionary, or others to speak to the group about different customs used in the celebration of Mass throughout the world.

Faith Development (_____min.)

3. The most effective way of developing an understanding of the Mass is to involve the young people in preparing for a Mass they will join in together. After reading section one on page 72, ask for volunteers to outline on the board the Introductory Rites and the Liturgy of the Word. Have a lectionary available, as well as a hymnal or missalette. Invite volunteers to plan a Mass, choosing the readings, sung acclamations, and appropriate songs. Practice with them the responses to the readings. Ask another group to prepare petitions for the General Intercessions.

   Invite volunteers to respond to the final two questions on page 72.

4. Read together section two on page 73 about the Liturgy of the Eucharist. Ask the young people why they think Jesus chose bread and wine for the Eucharist. (They are basic elements for human nourishment and were part of the Passover celebration.) Remind them that Jesus also called Himself the Bread of Life and the true Vine.

   In preparation for Mass, invite the young people to think about their own lives—things that are "broken" and need to be put together, their needs, hopes, and joys. They might write these on slips of paper and use them as part of the preparation of the gifts.

5. Read together the Eucharistic Prayer that will be used at Mass. Challenge the young people to find words of praise and thanksgiving to God in this prayer. Talk about what we are remembering in the Eucharistic Prayer, especially the narrative in which Jesus institutes the Eucharist. Show how the Eucharistic Prayer ends with the Great Amen, which should be proclaimed by all. Point out the significance of the Lord's Prayer and the

sign of peace that we offer. Talk about what the priest does during the Lamb of God: our Eucharistic Bread is broken so that it may be shared in Communion.

6. Have a volunteer read the *Do You Know* section on page 73. Then read section three together on page 74. Talk about what it means to "go in peace" and what it means "to love and serve the Lord." Ask the young people to think of one thing they will do to love and serve the Lord as they are sent forth from Mass.

   Have volunteers choose a "going forth" song to sing at the end of Mass.

   Assign *Church Teachings,* and *Things to Think About* for review and study.

Faith Response/Decision (_____min.)

7. If it is possible, after the group has completed its preparations, have a priest celebrate Mass with the group. If it is not possible to have a Mass, gather the group in a quiet, peaceful atmosphere. Invite them to reflect silently on *Things to Share.* After a few minutes, have them stand and pray the Lord's Prayer together.

8. For further prayerful reflections, encourage the young people to use pages 26–27 of the *One Faith, One Lord* Journal.

 # 12 The Sacrament of Reconciliation

Goal: To appreciate the sacrament of mercy and forgiveness

Adult Background

When Jesus raised Lazarus from the dead, He performed a miracle. When He forgave Zacchaeus and the woman caught in adultery, He restored them to life. For those who have eyes to see, forgiveness is "the greatest and most incomprehensible miracle of God's love" (Karl Rahner).

The Church freely offers us, in the sacrament of Reconciliation, an opportunity to encounter Christ and experience the miracle of "your sins are forgiven. Go in peace."

Reconciliation raises us from the death of sin, which alienates us from God, our true selves, and those around us. It restores us to healthful and harmonious relationships.

By all Gospel accounts, reconciliation is an occasion of great joy—both for the Forgiver and the forgiven one. Likewise, in the Church, this sacrament is intended to be a joyful celebration of homecoming. "It is not judgment, blame, criticism or punishment that we should encounter in the Sacrament of Reconciliation, but the offer of understanding love and friendship" (Bishop Joseph Gerry, "We Are Called to Conversion").

When we make this offer available to youth, whether in parish, diocesan, or retreat settings, we are extending Jesus' ministry of healing love. Young people sense the reality of sin, within and without. They struggle with dishonesty, disrespect, laziness, violence, and the failure to esteem themselves (bodies and spirits) as well as others.

They need to be reassured that no matter what they have done or failed to do, Jesus is inviting them personally to come to Him and unburden their hearts. When they choose to be reconciled, they are allowing Christ to do for them what He did for Zacchaeus and the woman caught in adultery. They are opening themselves to the miracle of "Go in peace, your sins are forgiven."

Preparing the Session

Read through the entire session and familiarize yourself with the annotations provided, as well as materials needed, if any. *Determine what your specific learning objectives are for this session.* Adapt the following plans according to your gifts, the needs of your young people, and the time period provided.

It may be helpful to plan the number of minutes you wish to give each section of the lesson. There are spaces provided below for this purpose. Doing this will insure that you will cover *completely* the material for the session.

Now, look at all the photographs and illustrations in this session. Choose those that you want to highlight as integral and most appropriate to your specific lesson plan. Be sure to preview any audio-visuals you may have selected.

Experience/Reflection (_____min.)

1. Talk about the dreams and plans that all of us have. Read pages 76–77 together and allow time for the group to respond to the questions. Discuss possible consequences or effects certain choices will have. Ask: How does one go about making important decisions? Then ask the group to reflect on the final question before responding.

Faith Development (_____min.)

2. Read together section one on pages 78–79 together. Have each part of Luke's Gospel roleplayed as it comes up in the reading. After reading, have volunteers outline on the board the choices and the consequences made by both the father and the son in the story. Point out the

fact that Jesus wants us to know of the Father's unconditional love for each one of us. An understanding of this love can do so much for those young people who experience doubt about their own self-worth. Help the young people to answer the final question of section one.

3. Read section two on pages 79–80. Discuss: "Sin is always a personal choice." Then ask:
   - What is conscience? (the ability we have to decide whether an action is right or wrong)
   - What is conversion? (turning back to God)
   - What is the difference between mortal and venial sin? (mortal sin is a complete break in our relationship with God.)

   Be sure the young people understand the conditions for mortal sin. Point out the *Do You Know* on page 78. Then ask:
   - What is temptation? (It is a tendency to sin; it is not a sin.)

Faith Response/Decision (_____min.)

4. Help the young people understand how to make an examination of conscience. Remind them that it is a way to reflect on the choices we have made, and how we can do better in the future.

5. Read together section three on pages 80–81. Go over carefully the ways to celebrate the sacrament of Reconciliation. If possible, invite a priest from the parish to talk to the group about Reconciliation.

   Have the young people memorize the Act of Contrition on page 122 of the *Prayers and Practices* section of their text (if they have not already done so). Help them to understand the meaning of absolution, the words of forgiveness spoken by the priest. Then help them to answer the final questions of section three on page 81.

   Then assign *Church Teachings* on page 81 for review and home study. Point out the last statement concerning the seal of confession.

6. Gather the group in quiet. Invite them to become very still. If possible, play quiet background music. Then ask them to reflect on *Things to Think About* and *Things to Share* on page 81. Allow several minutes for this, then close by inviting the group to pray silently, "Lord Jesus, have mercy on me a sinner." Remember that your positive and joyful attitude toward the sacrament will do much to help the young people.

7. For further prayerful reflection, encourage the young people to use pages 28–29 of the *One Faith, One Lord* Journal.

13 Living God's Law

Goal: To understand the basis of Christian morality

Adult Background

As Christians we can easily lose sight of Jesus' Jewish heritage. But in sharing our understanding of God's law, we need to see Jesus in the historical context of His own faith.

The faithfulness of Jesus to the Torah (the whole law of Judaism) is praised by many Jewish scholars and recognized in Israeli history texts. Two centuries ago Rabbi Jakob Emden wrote that Jesus had "consolidated Moses' Torah with all his strength" and had verified the importance of observing God's law.

When some Pharisees accused Jesus of breaking the divine law, He replied that it was not God's command but their oral interpretation that He rejected. (See Mark 7:1–13.)

Jesus, the new Moses, teaches His followers to fulfill the spirit of the law. He chides some of the Pharisees for failing to obey "the really important teachings of the Law, such as justice and mercy and honesty. These you should practice, without neglecting the others" (Matthew 23:23).

By His teaching and example, Jesus requires His followers to "keep the commandments." He summarizes the spirit of the Ten Commandments by stating God's Law of Love. And He promises that those who obey the law and teach others to do likewise "will be great in the Kingdom of heaven" (Matthew 5:19).

The Commandments were for Jesus and are for us an integral aspect of the Way. They remind us of our need to put God first in our lives, to be reverent, faithful, honest, respectful, nonviolent, and just. They point the way to a world in which women and men, children and parents, neighbors and communities are restored to right relationships.

In her practical wisdom, Saint Teresa of Avila noted, "We cannot be sure if we are loving God, although we may have good reasons for believing that we are, but we can know quite well if we are loving our neighbor" (*The Prison of Love:* Selections from St. Teresa of Avila).

Preparing the Session

Read through the entire session and familiarize yourself with the annotations provided, as well as materials needed, if any. *Determine what your specific learning objectives are for this session.* Adapt the following plans according to your gifts, the needs of your young people, and the time period provided.

It may be helpful to plan the number of minutes you wish to give each section of the lesson. There are spaces provided below for this purpose. Doing this will insure that you will cover *completely* the material for the session.

Now, look at all the photographs and illustrations in this session. Choose those that you want to highlight as integral and most appropriate to your specific lesson plan. Be sure to preview any audio-visuals you may have selected.

Experience/Reflection (_____min.)

1. Decorate the room with signs such as the following:
   - Detour. Unsafe bridge.
   - No trespassing. Watchdog.
   - Make sure campfire is completely out.

   Have the young people react to these and suggest other signs that warn and protect us. Discuss why such signs and rules are important for people's well-being.
2. Point out the questions at the bottom of page 84 in preparation for this session. The opening picture depicts John Paul II addressing the General Assembly of the United Nations in New York City. He was

invited to do so because he is a recognized moral leader as well as a temporal sovereign in the world. Have a volunteer read page 85. Discuss both the young people's need for, and their objections to, rules. Ask them to put their thoughts into writing on the page. Then discuss the closing questions, especially the problem of freedom and law. Allow time for a thorough discussion. Then preview the three main points of this session.

Faith Development (_____min.)

3. Use the above discussion to introduce section one on page 86. After reading this section, ask the group to explain what a covenant is. Ask:
   - What is the difference between a covenant and any other agreement? (It is a promise between God and people to be faithful to each other.)
   - What did the people promise God? (to obey the commandments.)
   - What did God promise the people? (They would live in freedom, justice, and peace.)
4. Go over the first three commandments with the group. Help them to see that each of these commandments deals with an individual's relationship with God.
5. Allow time for the group to read section two on pages 87–88. Then form several groups. Assign a commandment to each group. The task is to apply the commandment to situations and attitudes in their own lives. Share these situations. Then discuss the experience:
   - What does this activity tell us about the commandments? (It shows that they are applicable to our lives.)
   - What two relationships do the commandments focus on? (Love of God and love of neighbor)
   - Is it possible to love God without loving our neighbor? (We cannot say that we love God and then ignore our neighbor; by loving our neighbor, we

are showing our love for God.) If time allows, the group may want to create a *Commandment Chart,* listing each commandment and describing how that commandment should be kept.

6. Read section three on pages 88–89. Then have volunteers do a dramatic reading of Luke 10:25–28. Discuss what it means to love one's neighbor as oneself. Then ask: Who is your neighbor? Invite the young people to read the beautiful story of the Good Samaritan (Luke 10:30–37) as noted in *Do You Know.* Tell them that they will refer to this story again in the near future. Assign *Church Teachings* for home study and review.

Faith Response/Decision (_____min.)

7. Create an atmosphere of quiet reflection. Ask the young people to respond in their journals to *Things to Think About* and *Things to Share.* If time allows, invite volunteers to share their reflections.
8. For further prayerful reflection, encourage the young people to use pages 30–31 of the *One Faith, One Lord* Journal.

14 Jesus' Way of Loving

Goal: To reflect on a life of Christian virtue

Adult Background

Most of us would be tempted to buy a book called *Eight Ways to Be Happy.* But if the author propagated a gospel of self-love and material success at any price, we might realize that our money was not well spent.

Jesus has already made us a gift of the Eight Ways; we find them in Matthew's Gospel (5:3–10). Jesus gives us His word that we will be happy (blessed) when we learn to live by the virtues He personified. Taken together, the Beatitudes are a detailed portrait of Christ. They reveal who He was and who we are to be. They instruct us on how we are to fulfill the spirit of the Law of Love. They are a challenge to take a giant step toward freedom.

When Jesus proclaimed the Eight Ways from the mountain top, He spoke to the crowds in a formula that would have been familiar to them. Many listeners would have known by heart the psalmist's lesson, "Happy is he who has regard for the lowly and the poor" (41:2), as well as Proverbs' "Happy are those who keep my ways" (8:33). They would have recognized that the Eight Ways called them to a high ethical standard. They were amazed at the authority of the Teacher who affirmed their potential for spiritual maturity.

The Beatitudes imply that we are all, by God's grace, capable of heroic virtue. They require us to live simply, entrust our security to God, and identify with those who are struggling simply to live.

They require us to obey the will of God, treat others with kindness, and avoid lording it over others. They require us to be repentant, merciful, and just; to be peaceable and makers of peace; to have undivided hearts; and to be undaunted by whatever we suffer for Jesus' sake.

The Beatitudes are a trumpet blast from the Lord, rousing us to strive for the sanctity that is rightly ours. Like the Magnificat, they challenge us to change the world and to "lift up the lowly." In teaching the Eight Ways to young people, we prepare them to become living portraits of Love.

Preparing the Session

Read through the entire session and familiarize yourself with the annotations provided, as well as materials needed, if any. *Determine what your specific learning objectives are for this session.* Adapt the following plans according to your gifts, the needs of your young people, and the time period provided.

It may be helpful to plan the number of minutes you wish to give each section of the lesson. There are spaces provided below for this purpose. Doing this will insure that you will cover *completely* the material for the session.

Now, look at all the photographs and illustrations in this session. Choose those that you want to highlight as integral and most appropriate to your specific lesson plan. Be sure to preview any audio-visuals you may have selected.

Experience/Reflection (_____min.)

1. Point out the questions at the bottom of page 90. Then begin this session by focusing on the young people's ideas about happiness. Form small groups. Have each group write five statements that express its view of a way to happiness. Then have each group present its statements. Discuss:
   ● What do you think happiness is?
   ● How do you think happiness can be achieved?
   ● How are freedom and happiness connected? (We must be free in order to be happy.)
   ● How are rules and happiness connected? (Rules are made to protect the rights of people, thereby enabling

them to pursue happiness in freedom.)

2. Read together page 91. Compare this material with the results of the groups' questions. Have the young people write on the page their individual answers to what they think happiness is. If time allows, use the final questions on page 91 in preparation for the discussion about the Beatitudes.

Faith Development (_____min.)

3. Ask the young people to read section one on page 92. Create a word-picture of the scene: the crowds around Jesus on the hillside over the lake; people from every walk of life, the rich, the poor; those who have come to criticize; those who have come to be encouraged. Then Jesus begins to speak. Now have someone who has prepared in advance read the Beatitudes aloud, slowly and reverently. Ask:
   - How do you think different people in the crowd might have responded to Jesus?
   - What image of God do the Beatitudes create?

   Invite volunteers to respond to the final question on page 92.

4. Section two on page 93 presents the "new commandment" of Jesus: His disciples must love one another as Jesus has loved them. Read this section together. If time allows have the group read from their Bibles Matthew 5:38–48 (point out that this is also part of Jesus' Sermon on the Mount), and John 15:1–17.

   If time allows, talk about the meaning of love of enemies. How do you think Jesus' disciples reacted to the new commandment? What does our society and our media seem to value more: power over enemies or love of enemies?

5. Discuss with the group how the photographs on pages 92–93 reflect Jesus' new commandment. Encourage them to begin to create a "gallery" of photos and articles about "Beatitude people" who are living according to Jesus' new commandment.

6. Have the group silently read section three on page 94. Then provide materials for them to create Gospel message banners of faith, hope, and love to display in the room. Some suggestions might be Matthew 11:28; Mark 8:29; Luke 14:27; John 15:12.

   A discussion of the "theological virtues" (see *Do You Know* on page 94) may be difficult for young people striving to grow in the spiritual life. Help them to see that a virtuous life, far from being a boring life, is a life filled with challenge and commitment. As the text points out, persons of faith, hope, and love are people who are willing to risk generosity and sacrifice, and not compromise Christian values. How do we grow in a life of virtue? Through the sacraments, prayer, and an active life in the Church community.

7. Assign *Church Teachings* and *Words to Remember* on page 95 for home study and review. Those who wish to read more of the Sermon on the Mount should be encouraged to do so.

Faith Response/Decision (_____min.)

8. Create a quiet atmosphere and invite the group to reflect quietly on *Things to Think About* and *Things to Share* and to make their journal entries. Close with the Prayer of Saint Francis. If possible, use the recording of the musical version of this prayer from *Glory and Praise* or other sources.

9. For further prayerful reflection, encourage the young people to use pages 32–33 of the *One Faith One Lord* Journal.

15 In the Service of Others

Goal: To understand the Christian mission of prayerful service

Adult Background

In his essay "The Good Samaritan," Thomas Merton reflects that the question "Who is my neighbor?" is an attempt to "draw the line." The lawyer who asks the question in the Gospel passage wants to know whom he should judge worthy of his loving service.

Jesus' parable intends to lead us beyond this habit of classifying people into those who deserve our care and those who do not. By his extravagant ministry to the Jewish victim, the Samaritan shows us what God's loving mercy looks like.

Mercy does not discriminate. It does not set limits or count the cost. It is filled with kindness. We are drawn to the merciful Samaritan, our beloved Christ figure. But Merton invites us to look more deeply into the parable. "In the end," he says, "it is Christ Himself who lies wounded by the roadside. It is Christ who comes by in the person of the Samaritan. And Christ is the bond, the compassion, and the understanding between them" *(Seasons of Celebration,* p. 181*)*

We can take this parable as a paradigm for the Works of Mercy by which the Church calls us to minister in Christ's name. As a Catholic community we have an admirable history of caring for the sick, providing for the poor, feeding the hungry, and coming to the aid of those who "lie wounded by the roadside."

Within the Church, organizations like Catholic Relief Services, Diocesan Human Services, Maryknoll, and the Dorothy Day soup kitchens provide a channel for us to serve our sisters' and brothers' corporal needs.

Catholic schools and counseling services, retreat programs and support groups, peace and justice organizations like Pax Christi and Network witness to the ways we can serve others' spiritual needs. When we do all these Works of Mercy with love, we show that we have heard Christ's promise: "I tell you, whenever you did this for one of the least ones of mine, you did it for me!" (from Matthew 25:40). We can identify ourselves with Christ who is in need, Christ who ministers, and Christ who is the bond of compassion.

Preparing the Session

Read through the entire session and familiarize yourself with the annotations provided, as well as materials needed, if any. *Determine what your specific learning objectives are for this session.* Adapt the following plans according to your gifts, the needs of your young people, and the time period provided.

It may be helpful to plan the number of minutes you wish to give each section of the lesson. There are spaces provided below for this purpose. Doing this will insure that you will cover *completely* the material for the session.

Now, look at all the photographs and illustrations in this session. Choose those that you want to highlight as integral and most appropriate to your specific lesson plan. Be sure to preview any audio-visuals you may have selected.

Experience/Reflection (_____min.)

1. Show the group a large map of Central America and help them locate El Salvador. Then read the story of Jean Donovan on page 97. Stress the fact that she was an ordinary young American woman who saw people suffering and felt she had to respond. Point out that El Salvador was in the middle of a terrible civil war, and between the two armies were people— men, women, and children who were suffering the effects of war: poverty, sickness, starvation, death. Stress that the missionaries were not there to support one side of the war or the other,

but to serve the people. Help the young people relate the story of Jean Donovan as they reflect on the questions at the bottom of page 96.

2. Allow time for a thoughtful group discussion of the closing questions on page 97. Point out to the young people that everyone might not be called to a choice similar in challenge and difficulty to Jean Donovan's, but we are all called to love and service in Jesus' name.

Faith Development (_____min.)

3. Begin section one by having a group of volunteers do a dramatic reading or act out the story of the Good Samaritan (Luke 10:25–37) and a second group do the same for the story of the poor widow (Mark 12:41–44). These two Gospel accounts are on page 98. Guide a discussion that develops two key points of Christian living:
   ● Every person is worth our attention, care, and respect; everyone is our "neighbor."
   ● If we give and serve the best we can, we have given our all. Then read the closing four paragraphs on page 98.

4. Read together section two on pages 99–100. Point out the Works of Mercy on page 99, then form two groups, "Corporal Works" and "Spiritual Works." Each group should discuss and suggest ways people their age can practice these works of mercy now. Point out that there are different ways people can be hungry and thirsty and that to "clothe the naked" might mean to find a warm coat for a poor person in winter. And while they will not be involved in physically "burying the dead," they can support and be present to those who have lost loved ones.

5. Ask whether the young people recognize the person in the photograph on page 100 (Mother Teresa of Calcutta, India). Describe the love and service she has given to the "poorest of Christ's poor."

6. Present the Laws of the Church in section three, page 100. Read the section together and help the young people see that each obligation is simply a reinforcement of the Law of Love. To follow Christ we need to lead lives of love, prayer (the sacraments, fasting), and service (the missionary work of the Church). Then assign the *Do You Know* on page 101 for silent reading and *Church Teachings* and *Words to Know* for review.

Help the young people to see that we can accomplish so much in our own individual parish communities. Remind them that the parish is the focal point of our Christian life and how important it is for each of us to be active in parish life.

Faith Response/Decision (_____min.)

7. After reading *Things to Think About* ask the group to find out what special outreach programs for the poor, the hungry, the homeless, etc. are operating in their parish and diocese. Perhaps the young people are aware of certain needs of people that are not being met and can propose a project to the parish.

8. Allow a time for quiet reflection on *Things to Share*, page 101. Then ask the group to share their thoughts. You might wish to involve the young people in a day of "vocation awareness." Reflect together on the different ministries that are available in our Church and to which God calls us. Single people, married couples, priests, and religious could be invited to join you on this day. Close the session with silent prayer on Micah 6:8 by writing in their journals.

9. For further prayerful reflection, encourage the young people to use pages 34–35 of the *One Faith, One Lord* Journal.

16 Life Everlasting

Goal: To reflect on the "last things" and the saints

Adult Background

Death can be scary for anyone. Think of the first time you experienced the death of a loved one—your first wake or funeral. To help young people understand the hope-filled tradition that is ours in the Catholic Church, look to Christ as the "master catechist" when approaching questions about the "last things." He transformed the fear and sadness of Martha and Mary in John's Gospel: "I am the resurrection and the life. Do you believe this?" Each of them responded, "Yes, Lord, I have *come to believe*." (See John 11:1–45.)

We are called to come to faith, too. It begins now, in this life, as we grow in our relationship with Christ. Young people guided on that journey of faith will have a solid foundation to explore the mystery of life and death. They will come to know what the funeral liturgy underscores for us: "Life is changed, not ended." Christ has conquered death once and for all.

Christ showed us the way to the Father. He is our resurrection and life. We express this central belief and our future with words rich in symbolic meaning. *Heaven,* for example, reminds us that God wants us to be in a loving relationship with God forever. Neither Scripture nor centuries of theological reflection have even attempted to describe in detail what heaven is like (see 1 Corinthians 2:9). The "last things" speak of the future in terms of relationship of love: heaven (everlasting union with God); hell (everlasting separation from God); judgment (the importance of expressing and acting on our love for God and others). The choice, certainly, is ours. But God never stops inviting us.

Reflect on the words of our faith community: "If God is for us, who can be against us?" (Romans 8:31); "There are many rooms in my Father's house, and I am going to prepare a place for you. You will be where I am" (from John 14:2-3). Love grows to its fulfillment in Christ. "The sadness of death gives way to the bright promise of immortality." This is the bright promise of Easter.

Preparing the Session

Read through the entire session and familiarize yourself with the annotations provided, as well as materials needed, if any. *Determine what your specific learning objectives are for this session.* Adapt the following plans according to your gifts, the needs of your young people, and the time period provided.

It may be helpful to plan the number of minutes you wish to give each section of the lesson. There are spaces provided below for this purpose. Doing this will insure that you will cover *completely* the material for the session.

Now, look at all the photographs and illustrations in this session. Choose those that you want to highlight as integral and most appropriate to your specific lesson plan. Be sure to preview any audio-visuals you may have selected.

Experience/Response (_____min.)

1. Point out the questions at the bottom of page 102. Ask: Do you have questions like these? Have the young people briefly write down any questions they have about death, and then put the questions aside for now.

   Read the story of young King Tutankhamen on page 103 and discuss what his tomb revealed about the early Egyptian beliefs about death and the afterlife. Discuss the questions at the end of page 103 and allow time for the group to think about what they would put in their "Egyptian tombs."

2. Now distribute drawing paper and felt-tipped pens or color pencils. Ask the

young people to picture in their minds what death means to them and to depict their view in a drawing, perhaps using color or a symbolic representation of their feelings about death. Invite volunteers to share their finished drawings.

Faith Development (_____min.)

3. Read together section one on page 104. Then have four volunteers enact the roles of Abraham, Sara, Jesus, and an early Christian. Each tells the others in his/her own words (and the whole group) what they believe about death and resurrection. For example:
   Abraham or Sara: I think our life goes on in our children. That's why it means so much to us that we are finally going to have a child.

4. Take time with the *Do You Know* on page 104. Ask the group to try to imagine this life that we know will be totally changed, transformed from a physical world to a spiritual one. Point out that "spirit" suggests freedom, energy, love, a "lightness of being" as a poet described it.
   Saint Paul is basically telling us that our resurrected life is so wonderful that we cannot even imagine what God has prepared for us. Invite the young people to reflect on the final questions of section one.

5. Before reading section two, have volunteers do a dramatic reading of the story of Lazarus from John 11:1–45. Then read page 105, stressing judgment, heaven, hell. Make sure the young people understand that hell is always the *free choice* of the individual. God never turns away from us. It is important that young people be prepared to examine the choices they make and that they recognize and face the consequences of their choices—whether good or bad.
   After the young people have reflected on and shared their ideas on the last statement of page 105, invite them to quietly reflect on the Apostles' Creed or the Nicene Creed found on page 120 in *Prayers and Practices*.

6. Read section three on page 106. It makes sense that this chapter on life everlasting and this book on our basic beliefs conclude with a reflection on Mary and her role in our life of faith.
   Mary's choices were always for God's will. Mary was the perfect follower of Jesus. The young people should know that they are not alone on their journey of faith—they are part of a faithful, hopeful, loving communion of saints in heaven and on earth.
   Invite the young people to choose a favorite saint or one of the saints listed on pages 118–119 from the liturgical calendar. Volunteers may wish to research the life of a particular saint and share how that person courageously followed the path to holiness.

7. Use *Church Teachings* for a deeper understanding of the whole session. Highlight the last two items concerning Mary's Immaculate Conception and Assumption. You may also wish to refer to numbers 16 and 17 on pages 114–115 in the *Faith Summary*. Assign *Words to Remember* for review.

Faith Response/Decision (_____min.)

8. Invite the young people to gather in prayer. Engage them in quiet discussion of the ideas suggested in *Things to Think About* and *Things to Share*. Then have them make their final journal entries responding to these ideas. Close with the prayer on page 107.
   If possible, the ideal way to close this final session would be with a Mass in which the above suggestions could become the basis of a dialogue homily or Prayers of the Faithful.

9. For further prayerful reflection, encourage the young people to use pages 36–37 of the *One Faith, One Lord* Journal. Invite them to look over all their journal entries to see how far they have journeyed in faith during their time together.

One Faith, One Lord

REVISED AND EXPANDED

A Study of Basic Catholic Belief

Rev. Msgr. John F. Barry

Official Theological Consultant
Rev. Edward K. Braxton, Ph.D., S.T.D.

William H. Sadlier, Inc.
9 Pine Street
New York, NY 10005–1002

Contents

1 OUR CATHOLIC ROOTS

How do we discover the meaning of life?

Where do you search for answers to life's questions?

EXPERIENCE: We are invited on a journey of discovery—to look for answers to our basic human questions. Faith will be our guide.

Imagine that you have been invited to participate in a program on the new cable station QUEST. On this program the most important question in your life will be answered. What question will you ask?

(Do not insist that these questions be shared.)

_____

_____

_____

Now imagine that you are a famous explorer and have just uncovered the stone on which is written the mystical Code of All Answers. Being an expert translator, you now know the answer to all of life's questions. Write down your translation here.

(Allow for creativity and humor.)

_____

_____

_____

Welcome to a new time of discovery! This book is filled with all kinds of wonderful questions—questions that help you to discover and explore life and its meaning.

It is also filled with pathways that can help us to answer life's questions and make sense out of life. These answers come from our Catholic roots.

Some questions may be yours right now. Others may be new to you. But how wonderful it is that you can ask these questions and begin to get real answers.

This book has been written especially for you. Use it and do not be afraid to ask your important questions. All questions are good. How else do we grow and learn the truth? You may be surprised at what you discover. So ... upward and onward!

1 Our Catholic faith helps us to discover the meaning of life.

Human beings have always asked questions about the meaning of life and the origin of the world. No other creatures on earth can do this. We ask, "Where do things come from?" "Why are things the way they are?" "What is the meaning of life?"

These are only some of the exciting questions that we can ask. For centuries, people have been trying to answer them and to make sense out of life. They have used many ways to find satisfying answers. These ways include:

- our ability to reason and think, to generate ideas;

- personal experiences;

- reaching out and exploring beyond everyday knowledge;

- searching deep within the human spirit, as well as listening to those with whom we live and work.

All of these ways of discovery are wonderful—but we human beings have found them limited. Reason and experience have never answered fully everything we need or want to know. They can only take us so far. We need something more. For Catholics, that something more is faith.

What is faith? **Faith** is not just another point of view; it is a whole new way of looking at life. It is a gift from God. Faith helps us to begin to see our lives and the world as God sees them.

A person of faith knows that there is more to life than can be seen. Through the eyes of faith, we know that God is near, closer than we can imagine, and that God is the source of all life.

Faith, of course, does not take the place of reason, personal experience, human searching, or learning from others. Faith builds on our human abilities and works through them. We know this from our experience. In fact, when we look around us, we see that some of the most creative and talented people are people of faith.

Faith is like a key that unlocks many doors. Our faith shows us answers we would most often be unable to discover by ourselves.

What difference do you think faith can make in a person's life?

Why do you think faith is called a gift?

2 Through faith we come to know God.

ASK: Do you have questions about God? What are they?

Human beings have always used their reason to know that there must be some higher Power at work in the world. When we look at ourselves and the universe around us, we realize that something so wonderful could not come into existence or happen by itself. So human beings search for an answer. They search for God.

In this search, people living many thousands of years ago thought they found the answer in nature. Some named gods at work in the terrifying clap of thunder, the flash of lightning, and the rumble of an earthquake. Others found their gods in the sun, moon, and stars.

You may have read the fascinating stories and myths of ancient religions, such as those of Greece and Egypt. In those religions, the gods were often pictured as animals or even as people, each in charge of some important part of life. But these creature-like gods were not the one true God. They did not satisfy human beings in their search for the higher Power at work in the world.

The question still remained: Who really is God? The fullest answer to this question could only come from God. We call this **revelation**: God's telling us about God's own Self. The word *revelation* means to make someone or something known.

At a chosen time in the history of the world, God wanted to make a special revelation to human beings. God did this through the Israelites, the ancient Jews. Some of the things they came to know and believe about God were:

- There is only one true God, not many gods.
- God is not part of nature; God created nature and all that exists.
- God is a loving and caring God.
- God is active in the world and in our lives.
- We are called into a close relationship with God and called to live as God's people in the world.

How do we respond to God's revelation? We try to live as persons of faith, especially by turning to God in prayer and worship. We do this alone in our **personal prayer**, or together with others in **communal prayer**. In praising and thanking God for the gift of our lives, we also ask God for help because we trust in God's love.

We also respond to God by living our faith and doing what God asks of us, taking care of ourselves, others, and the world around us. In all these ways we grow as people of faith.

What do we mean by the word *revelation?*

What do we believe about the one true God?

Left to right: temple columns, Tula, Mexico; sacred dragon, Hong Kong; woodcut of Atlas carrying the universe; Navajo sand painting

 In the Bible we read the story of God's dealings with our ancestors in faith.

The ancient Israelites were a nomadic people. Their wandering lifestyle did not allow them the time to describe in writing their special relationship with God. Written documents were not even a part of their culture and way of life. But they passed on by word of mouth in beautiful stories of faith all that God had done for them.

After many centuries, the Israelites finally wrote down the oral traditions that had been passed from generation to generation. They did this under God's guidance, or **inspiration**. These sacred writings were the beginning of the book we now call the **Bible**.

The word *Bible* means "book." But the Bible is much more than a book in the modern sense. The Bible is like a small library; it is a collection of seventy-three smaller books. And these are divided into two main parts:

- The **Old Testament** contains forty-six books. We read in them about the faith relationship between God and the Israelites, later called the Jews.

- The **New Testament** contains twenty-seven books. They are about Jesus Christ, the Son of God, His message and mission, and His first followers.

ASK: Why is the Bible so important to us?

Do You Know

The word *tradition* literally means "handed on." In our Church, tradition means the truths and beliefs, both written and oral, that have come to us from the time of Jesus and the apostles. These are found in the creeds and other important Church documents.

Examples of Church teachings from tradition: the Assumption of Mary, purgatory

Catholics have deep respect for the Bible because we believe it is God's word to us. It cannot be read as a science book or a modern history book. The Bible is a book about faith.

The Bible was written over many centuries and had many human authors. These authors used many different forms and styles of writing, including short stories, history, poetry, letters, and parables. Because the Bible was written so long ago and in these many different styles, we need to take time to study it carefully. Knowing the background of the human authors, the culture of the times, and the different forms and styles of writing permit us to better understand God's word.

When we read the Bible with faith, we meet God. God's word is a vital part of what it means to be a Catholic, to share in the beautiful faith life and **tradition** of our Church. What God did for our ancestors in faith, God continues to do for us. How wonderful it is to share in our Catholic roots and to explore why faith is so important in our lives!

What is the Bible?

Explain the two main parts of the Bible.

Left to right: page from Book of Joshua in Hebrew; page from Matthew's Gospel in Greek

STRESS these Church teachings. Assign for review and home study.

Church Teachings About Catholic Roots

- Faith is a gift of God. Through faith we have the ability to believe all that God reveals to us and respond to God.

- Revelation is God's sharing with us who God is and what God asks of us. It is not a set of statements; it is God making God's own Self known to us in love.

- God can be revealed to us in nature, human events, and people.

- Above all God is revealed in and through Jesus Christ. He is the fullest revelation of God to humanity.

Prayer

Journaling is a wonderful way to pray, and you can begin your own prayer journal by setting your thoughts down in a personal journal as you complete each chapter of this book. Ask God to be with you and guide you in your journaling.

Reflection and Action

Words to Remember

Find and define the following.

faith a gift of God that helps us see our lives and the world as God sees them.

_____

_____

revelation means to make someone or something known.

_____

_____

Bible God's word; the inspired writings of our faith.

_____

_____

Things to Think About

Faith is alive! It must be lived in action. We cannot just talk about what we believe.

What can you do to grow in faith? What will you do to open your mind and heart to God?

Things to Share

What do you think it means to share faith with people of different times and cultures? Ask people you trust to tell how faith has helped them at important times—good times as well as bad times.

Invite the young people to begin their prayer journals. Stress the confidentiality of journals.

2 GOD THE CREATOR

How did our universe come about?

Does science have answers? Does faith?

What questions do you have about life's origins?

Do you ever look at the stars—really look at them? An American writer named Emerson did, and these were his thoughts.

Imagine, he said, that instead of shining every night, the stars would shine only once in a thousand years. Think of the awe people would feel as they gazed for the first time on the star-filled night! Instead of the endless darkness the people had always known, they now would see millions and millions of stars in the sky.

How they would treasure the memory of that night! They would tell their children about it, and their children would tell their grandchildren and great-grandchildren. How happily they would recall the memory of that wondrous night when the veil of darkness was drawn aside, and they seemed to see the wonder of God.

Imagine that it is a clear and starlit night. You are standing on a beach looking up into the vastness of space.

How do you think a poet would describe this scene? How would a scientist? How would you?

(Point out that we approach the mysteries of our universe from

different points of view, different levels of experience.)

_____

_____

_____

_____

STRESS that the poet and scientist are equally valuable for different reasons.

1 God is the Creator of the universe.

Since the dawn of history, a question that has challenged men and women concerns the beginnings of the world—and the people in it. Where did the world come from? How did it start?

Throughout the ages, attempts to explain the origin of the world have been made by scientists, historians, philosophers, and religious believers. Each area of study has made unique and truthful contributions to our understanding. Each has helped us to ask important questions.

Science and social studies try to answer the questions "how" and "when" our world came into being. Reasonable people want to know the answers to such questions. And science furnishes some answers. As our technical abilities have grown over centuries, scientific theories about creation have changed and adapted, expanding our knowledge.

In addition to the questions "how" and "when," people also ask "who" and "why": Who created the universe? Why was it created? These are questions that can be answered only in faith. After all, no one witnessed creation—except God!

In the **Book of Genesis**, the first book of the Bible, we find the beautiful poem of creation. It is a simple, poetic story about the creation of the universe. In this story, God fashions the world in a spectacular way over a six-day period, the length of the Israelite work week. The authors of Genesis have God begin by creating light. "Let there be light," God says. God creates effortlessly—by the power of a word.

Then, according to Genesis, God made the dome of the heavens, the sky. God put the mighty waters into place, some above the heavens, some on the earth, "and the water that had come together God named 'sea.'" God alone created everything. On the seventh day, at the end of the work week, God was

pictured as doing what the Israelites did: God rested.
From Genesis 1:1–11

From their description of the creation, we can tell that the Genesis authors were not trying to answer questions of science, but questions of faith. For example, the word *day* used in the creation story does not mean twenty-four hours as we know them. A period of seven days is simply a framework for telling the story. Inspired by God and by the beauty and majesty of the world around them, the Genesis authors wished to teach some important **truths of faith**:

DISCUSS: the truths of faith we learn from Genesis.

- God alone created everything that is.

- The world and everything in it is good as created and affirmed by God.

- We can learn something about God from the things God has made: God is all powerful, all-loving, all-creative, all-good.

How wonderful is the story of creation, calling forth from us feelings of praise and reverence for the Creator!

Responding to the wonder of creation, what will you say to God?

NOTE: Allow time for private reflection.

12

2 God is the Creator of all life.

In the beautiful poem of creation in the Book of Genesis, we read that God created all life: the plants and the trees, the fish and the birds, and all animals. Then finally God said, "Let there be human beings made in God's image and likeness."
From Genesis 1:26

Just think—**made in God's image and likeness**! What do these words really mean for us? In a wonderful way they remind us that human beings, both women and men, are the crowning achievement of God's creation. No other creature or thing is made in the image of God. No other creature can think, choose, and love in the likeness of the Creator.

Being made in the image and likeness of God offers to each of us tremendous challenges. If we are to grow in God's image, then we must use our minds, make responsible choices, and open our hearts to love. When we look upon another human person or look deeply into ourselves, what we should see is a reflection of God our Creator.

The Book of Psalms is a book of prayers in the Bible. It contains many references to God as the Creator of everything, and to men and women as God's special creation. We read in Psalm 8:

> When I look at the sky, which you
>   have made,
>   at the moon and the stars,
>   which you set in their places—
> what are human beings, that you think
>   of them;
>   mere human beings, that you care for
>   them?
>
> Yet you made them inferior only to
>   yourself;
>   you crowned them with glory
>   and honor.
> From Psalm 8:3–5

There is more to the Genesis story of creation and the meaning of being made in God's image, as we shall see.

What does it mean for you to be made in the image and likeness of God?

NOTE: take time to go over the illustration below. Then have the young people go over *Helps to Understanding the Bible* on page 115.

GENESIS 42, 43   46

harm the boy, but you wouldn't listen. And now we are being paid back for his death." 23 Joseph understood what they said, but they did not know it, because they had been speaking to him through an interpreter. 24 Joseph left them and began to cry. When he was able to speak again, he came back, picked out Simeon, and had him tied up in front of them.

Joseph's Brothers Return to Canaan
25 Joseph gave orders to fill his brothers' packs with grain, to put each man's money back in his sack, and to give them food for the trip. This was done. 26 The brothers loaded their donkeys with the grain they had bought, and then they left. 27 At the place where they spent the night, one of them opened his sack to feed his donkey and found his money at the top of the sack. 28 "My money has been returned to me," he called to his brothers. "Here it is in my sack!" Their hearts sank, and in fear they asked one another, "What has God done to us?"
29 When they came to their father Jacob in Canaan, they told him all that had happened to them: 30 "The governor of Egypt spoke harshly to us and accused us of spying against his country. 31 'We are not spies,' we answered, 'we are honest men. 32 We were twelve brothers in all, sons of the same father. One brother is dead, and the youngest is still in Canaan with our father.' 33 The man answered, 'This is how I will find out if you are honest men: One of you will stay with me; the rest will take grain for your starving families and leave. 34 Bring your youngest brother to me. Then I will know that you are not spies, but honest men; I will give your brother back to you, and you can stay here and trade.'"
35 Then when they emptied out their sacks, every one of them found his bag of money; and when they saw the money, they and their father Jacob were afraid. 36 Their father said to

not bring Benjamin back to you, you can kill my two sons. Put him in my care, and I will bring him back."
38 But Jacob said, "My son cannot go with you; his brother is dead, and he is the only one left. Something might happen to him on the way. I am an old man, and the sorrow you would cause me would kill me."

*Joseph's Brothers Return to Egypt
with Benjamin*
43 The famine in Canaan got worse. 2 and when the family of Jacob had eaten all the grain which had been brought from Egypt, Jacob said to his sons, "Go back and buy a little food for us."
3 Judah said to him, "The man sternly warned us that we would not be admitted to his presence unless we had our brother with us. 4 If you are willing to send our brother with us, we will go and buy food for you. 5 If you are not willing, we will not go, because the man told us we would not be admitted to his presence unless our brother was with us."
6 Jacob said, "Why did you cause me so much trouble by telling the man that you had another brother?"
7 They answered, "The man kept asking about us and our family, 'Is your father still living? Do you have another brother?' We had to answer his questions. How could we know that he would tell us to bring our brother with us?"
8 Judah said to his father, "Send the boy with me, and we will leave at once. Then none of us will starve to death. 9 I will pledge my own life, and you can hold me responsible for him. If I do not bring him back to you safe and sound, I will always bear the blame. 10 If we had not waited so long, we could have been there and back twice by now."
11 Their father said to them. "If that is how it has to be, then take the best products of the land in your packs as a present for the governor: a little resin, a little honey, spices, pistachio nuts, and almonds. 12 Take with you also twice as much money, because

— **Book of the Bible**

— **Verse number**

— **Verse**

— **Chapter number**

— **Passage titles:** titles added to break up the chapters, not the actual words of the Bible

— **Bible passage:** a section of a chapter made up of a number of verses

How to Find Your Way in the Bible

It is easy to find your way in the Bible once you know how. There are seventy-three *books* in the Bible. Each book is divided into *chapters*, and each chapter into *verses*. Thus, a Bible reference such as Genesis 1:1–11 means: the Book of Genesis, chapter one, verses one to eleven.

3 God calls us to share in the work of creation.

Life is a gift. God freely gave life to humanity. In a wondrous way, God created us male and female, partners with God and equal partners with each other.

According to the creation story of Genesis, God spoke to the first human beings. In the story they are called Adam and Eve, and they stand for all humanity. God said to them, "Have many children, so that your descendants will live all over the earth and bring it under their control. I am putting you in charge of the fish, the birds, and all the wild animals" (Genesis 1:28). In other words, God was inviting human beings to join in a partnership in the work of and care for creation.

God entrusted creation to the care of the human race. We are to find the best use for everything God created. This means several things:

- We are to respect and care for our environment. The earth, the air, and the water cannot be polluted. They are for all creatures.

- We must develop and use our talents and abilities to be effective partners with God. When we improve our world and conserve its resources, we build a better life for all.

God's creation is truly a wonder. But the work of creation is not finished. As partners with God, we continue this work in many ways— for example, by planting crops, feeding the world, exploring the whole universe, and making the glory of God's name known throughout all creation.

How will you be a partner with God in the work of creation?

ASK: What does it mean to you to know that you have a responsibility for creation?

14

Church Teachings About Creation

- The Church respects science and its insights, which help men and women have a deeper understanding of creation.

- God created the universe. The scientific theory that the world was gradually formed over millions of years is compatible with Church teaching. Science and religion are not enemies but should be partners in the search for truth.

- God created human beings, too. Each person has an immortal soul and is special and unique. But our Church does not teach us "how" God created humankind. This is a question for science to answer. That is why the scientific theory of human evolution is compatible with our Catholic beliefs.

- The gift of faith helps us to believe that God is the Source of all creation.

Prayer

Use the beautiful words of Psalm 8 as your prayer. Slowly pray each phrase and each line. Now share your thoughts and feelings with God. You may wish to write them in your journal.

Reflection and Action

Words to Remember

Find and define the following:

creation story a simple poetic story of creation found in Genesis.

image and likeness of God means that we can think, choose, love as God does.

Book of Genesis the first book of the Bible.

Things to Think About

The authors of the Book of Genesis never could have dreamed that we would know so much today about our world. They had no idea of outer space, interplanetary travel, or the marvelous microscopic world of the cell. But their insights of faith are more valid today than ever.

What marvels of God's creation speak to you?

What does creation teach us of God's love, power, and humor?

These reflections can also be entered in the prayer journals.

Things to Share

At which times of the day are you especially aware of God's creative power?

How will you share with others in the responsibility to care for and develop God's creation?

Share this prayer with others: Lord, I sense Your presence in all creation, the large and small, the cosmic and the microscopic. Thank You, Lord, for all that You have made. Amen.

3 THE FALL AND THE PROMISE

Why is there suffering in our world?

Does faith help us to answer our questions about good and evil?

EXPERIENCE: When a tragedy occurs, a person's hope and courage can be restored by the care and concern of others.

The first day! Erica had not thought of it for a long time. But she could recall it as if it were yesterday. She remembered how ill she was the day she walked into the hospital.

Her mind went back even further to another day when she had first asked Kurt so innocently, "How do drugs make you feel?" That was the beginning of Erica's nightmare. The last straw was when she tried to steal from her friends at school to support her drug habit.

With professional and family help, Erica went through a painful and lengthy period of withdrawal. All that was behind her now. Hope had been held out to her, and the promised new day and new start were now a reality. Erica picked up her suitcase and ran out to meet her family.

Like all of us do, Erica had been looking for happiness, but she looked in the wrong place. Her story reminds us that many things can threaten happiness, such as a broken friendship, an illness, hurt feelings, or some human tragedy. But if we are determined, as Erica seems to have been, we can overcome our difficulties, too.

Can you give an example of a wrong or harmful choice? What were the consequences?

_____

_____

_____

_____

Why do you think we sometimes choose to do things that are not right for us?

Where do you find hope in the midst of difficulties or sadness?

ASK: How important was the support Erica received from her family and friends?

17

Evil has its origins in human beings, not in God.

STRESS the underlined copy.

We do not have to live very long to know that pain and disappointment are a part of life. Human beings suffer from the effects of hatred, greed, and selfishness. The daily news is filled with reports of violence, suffering, and death, so often brought about by human beings themselves.

Life is a mixture of good and bad. People may have high hopes; they also may have shattered dreams. People know happiness; they also experience sorrow. <u>Why is life both beautiful and tragic?</u>

<u>The writers of the Book of Genesis asked the same puzzling question.</u> As an answer, the inspired authors told an imaginary story in which they tried to explain the origins of evil in the world. The main characters of the story were called **Adam** and **Eve**, the names traditionally given to the first man and woman. Evil, the authors wanted to teach us, has been a part of the human experience from the very beginning.

According to the story, the first couple lived in a beautiful garden. It was the Lord God's gift to them. They had all they needed for a happy life. For their own good, God said to them, "You may eat the fruit of any tree in the garden, except the tree that gives knowledge of what is good and what is bad. You may not eat the fruit of that tree; if you do, you will die the same day."

Then the spirit of evil appeared. Disguised as a serpent, it spoke first to the woman and said, "Did God really tell you not to eat from any tree in the garden?"

The woman replied, "We may eat the fruit of any tree in the garden except the tree in the middle of it. God told us not to eat the fruit of that tree or even touch it; if we do, we will die."

The serpent answered, "That's not true; you will not die. God said that because God knows that when you eat it, you will be like God and know what is good and what is bad."

The woman saw how beautiful the tree was and how good its fruit would be to eat, and she thought how wonderful it would be to become like God. So she took some of the fruit and ate it. Then she gave some to her husband, and he also ate it.

<u>By their own actions, human beings chose evil over good. They rejected the wonderful gifts that God had given them. Sin had entered into our world.</u> To dramatize this fact, the inspired authors of Genesis ended the story with God sending the couple from the garden. The man and the woman had broken their friendship with God and had lost the right to be there.
From Genesis 3:1–23

What do you think about the choice the couple made in the story?

NOTE: This story is not an eye-witness account. It is intended to teach a religious truth through symbols.

Church Teachings: Fall and Promise

- Sin entered the world through human choice.

- The first sin of the human race is called original sin. Every human being is born with and suffers from the effects of this sin.

- Jesus Christ is the "new Adam" whose obedience unto death saves us from sin.

- Jesus Christ fulfills all God's promises and frees us to share in God's life and love, which we call grace.

2 All of us suffer from the effects of original sin.

The story of Adam and Eve taught very important truths of faith. It was the kind of drama that was easy for the ancient Israelites to remember and understand. We have come to see that the story was built on symbols with which these people were very familiar.

Imagine that you lived with the ancient Israelites. If you had, you would have been living in or near a desert. So you would know how special it was to be anywhere near a garden!

The Genesis authors wanted to show God's love for the first human beings by placing them in a **garden** filled with running water, lush plants, and fruit-laden trees. The garden was a symbol of happiness and of God's grace. **Grace** is a sharing in the life and love of God. Having this gift of grace means that God's own life and love are in us.

Many other symbols were used in the story as well. The **serpent** was a symbol of evil. The Israelites worshiped only the one true God, but their pagan neighbors often worshiped serpents. **Eating the fruit of the forbidden tree** was another symbol. It helped the Israelites to appreciate the power they had as human beings to choose between good and evil. **Being sent out of the garden** symbolized turning away from God and the loss of God's grace.

The story of the garden dramatizes how close the relationship is between God and men and women. But it also dramatizes how that relationship is shattered by sin.

DISCUSS the elements of sinful choices.

19

The elements of sin are all present in the story:

- temptation comes, and we are led to believe that a certain choice will bring us happiness;
- we are attracted by a "false good" and give in to temptation;
- having made a deliberate choice, we must live out the consequences of that choice.

The first couple in the story failed to prove worthy of God's trust. They did not respond gratefully or lovingly to God. They turned away, selfishly choosing what they wanted rather than what God wanted for them. We call this first sin of humankind **original sin**. By using this term, we refer to the sin that affects all human beings. We all share in sinfulness, and at birth, we are born into a world in which evil is a reality.

For those who are ready to understand, this simple story from Genesis can offer so much truth about our relationship with God and our need to be brought back into the life of grace. This is what it means to be redeemed.

What do we mean by original sin?

Do You Know

One of the greatest books of the Old Testament is the Book of the prophet Isaiah. The prophet spoke of someone who would come and understand our human selfishness and pride. This person would relieve the tragedy of sin and restore our identity as true sons and daughters of God. The prophet described this person as the **suffering servant**. Today we use Isaiah's words to describe Christ. "My devoted servant will bear the punishment of many" (from Isaiah 53:11).

3 God promised to send the world a Savior.

STRESS: God did not leave us to face evil alone.

The Genesis story of Adam and Eve did not end in despair. It ended on a note of hope and mercy. The inspired authors of Genesis knew that God had never abandoned humankind. In the story, God had promised that sin and evil would not triumph: that the offspring of Adam and Eve would one day crush the head of the serpent (Genesis 3:15). Christians believe that this promise was carried out by Jesus Christ our Savior. Jesus brought the final victory over sin and evil.

People knew that the journey back to a full and loving relationship with God was going to be a difficult one. Even though people would still turn to sin, God would forgive them and never stop loving them.

When people felt low and hopeless, God encouraged them. God sent special people called **prophets** to speak for God and to remind people that God had not forgotten them. God promised to send them the Messiah, the Anointed One, who would restore their relationship with God.

Christians believe that Christ fulfills all God's promises. Saint Paul identifies Christ as the

"new Adam" — the new Man. Through His obedience unto death, Jesus became the Savior of the world. We must respond to the salvation that Jesus has won for us. Through Jesus, we are restored to God's life and love.

The New Testament tells us about Jesus' life, death, and resurrection. Through His life, death, and resurrection, Jesus Christ saves us from evil and shares God's life and love in a human way. That is why at Mass we often acclaim this great mystery of faith: "Dying you destroyed our death, rising you restored our life. Lord Jesus, come in glory."

NOTE: Evil exists in the world because of sin. Through Jesus Christ we are saved from sin and freed to share God's life and love.

Prayer

Use the words that we often proclaim at Mass. Make them your prayer this week. "Dying you destroyed our death, rising you restored our life. Lord Jesus, come in glory."

In your journal, you may wish to reflect on these questions: What can I do to lessen pain and evil in the world? What can I do to share with others the hope of my Christian faith?

Reflection and Action

Words to Remember

Find and define the following.

original sin The first sin of humankind that affects all human beings.

_____

grace a sharing in the life and love of God.

_____

_____

garden (symbol in Genesis) is used as a symbol of happiness and God's grace.

_____

_____

Things to Think About

What evidence of original sin can you find in today's headlines and newscasts?

Why do you think Jesus is a sign of hope?

Things to Share

A popular error is that the fruit eaten by Adam and Eve was an apple. You know that no specific fruit is mentioned in the Genesis story. In fact, the story is filled with symbols like this. Would you be able to share with others what these symbols stand for? What would you say?

4 JESUS, THE PROMISE FULFILLED

Who are you? Who do you want to be?

Are the answers to these questions the same for you?

If you were to find a lost wallet on the street, what might you discover in it? What might it contain? Perhaps it would include photographs, a personal ID card, a driver's license, credit cards, tickets to sporting or theater events, a health club membership card—even money! Using these items, what could you say about the owner of the wallet?

As you look at these ideas, what do they tell you about the *real* person who owns this wallet?

_____

_____

_____

What are the things that you carry in your wallet or with you? What would these items tell others about you?

_____

_____

_____

Our faith tells us that Jesus is so important for our lives. But who is Jesus? How can we begin to describe who He is? Where do we turn for clues in our search for Him?

EXPERIENCE: We have to know who we are in order to have direction in our lives.

1 Jesus is the promised Savior.

STRESS the underlined copy.

Over many centuries God prepared the people of Israel for the fulfillment of God's promises. The Old Testament prophets reminded them that God never stopped loving them and that their relationship with God would be restored by the Promised One. Who would he be? How would his coming be known? What would his relationship with God be?

Little by little the prophets gave some clues about the Promised One of God. For example, he would be from the family of David, the greatest king of Israel, and would be born in Bethlehem. He would be called God's anointed one, the **Messiah**. He would be not only a great leader, but also the Savior.

Knowing the message of the prophets, the first Christians could see that the prophets' clues about the Promised One were fulfilled in Jesus Christ. They preached this Good News and even wrote down their beliefs in the pages of the New Testament.

According to Luke's Gospel, about two thousand years ago an angel of God was sent to a young Jewish girl who lived in the town of Nazareth. Her name was Mary, and she was promised in marriage to a man named Joseph. After greeting her, the angel said, "Don't be afraid, Mary; God has been gracious to you. You will give birth to a son, and you will name him Jesus. He will be great and will be called the Son of the Most High God."

Deeply troubled by this message, Mary said to the angel, "I am a virgin. How can this be?"

Then the angel told her something astonishing: "The Holy Spirit will come upon you, and God's power will rest upon you. For this reason the holy child will be called the Son of God."

What exciting news Mary received! She would be a virgin mother by the power of the Holy Spirit. Her child would be the **Son of God**. According to Luke's Gospel, which tells the story from Mary's point of view, Mary totally accepted what God wanted her to do. Mary said to the angel, "I am the Lord's servant; may it happen to me as you have said." From Luke 1:26–38

These events in Luke's Gospel form what we call the **Annunciation**. It is the story of the angel's visit to Mary, telling her that she would be the Mother of God by the power of the Holy Spirit.

Matthew's Gospel describes in a different way how God's promises were finally fulfilled. The story is told from Joseph's point of view. The events of the Annunciation to Mary are not mentioned.

According to Matthew's Gospel, an angel came to Joseph in a dream and spoke these assuring words: "Joseph, descendant of David, do not be afraid to take Mary as your wife. For it is by the Holy Spirit that she has conceived. She will have a son, and you will name him Jesus—because he will save his people from their sins." From Matthew 1:18–23

From these two Gospel accounts, which you may wish to read in their entirety in the Bible, it is clear that the early Christians believed that Jesus was the Promised Savior. God was going to fulfill the promise in a way that no one expected. The Promised One would not only be a great man; He would be God's own Son as well.

Why do you think Mary and Joseph responded as they did to God's message? Would you?

24

The Annunciation, 15th-century painting by Domenico Veneziano

ASSIGN for review and home study.

Church Teachings About Jesus

- Jesus, the Messiah, is the Promised Savior. *Messiah* is a word that means Christ, or the Anointed One of God. That is why we say that Jesus is the Christ.

- There are three divine Persons in one God: the Father, the Son, and the Holy Spirit. We call this the Blessed Trinity.

- God the Father is the First Person of the Blessed Trinity; God the Son is the Second Person of the Blessed Trinity; and God the Holy Spirit is the Third Person of the Blessed Trinity.

- The Second Person of the Trinity became flesh, became one of us: Jesus Christ.

- Jesus Christ is both human and divine.

- Jesus came to announce that the Kingdom of God was at hand.

DISCUSS the two gospel accounts on page 24. How are they the same? How do they differ?

2 Jesus Christ is both human and divine.

Where do we discover the truth about Jesus, who He really is? First we turn to the writings of the New Testament, especially the Gospels. The word **gospel** means "good news." The Good News of Jesus Christ is proclaimed in the four Gospel accounts of Matthew, Mark, Luke, and John. These accounts were written after the life, death, and resurrection of Jesus. They are God's word and also express the faith of the early Church community.

Although they are not biographies, the Gospels are a rich source of information about Jesus. They give us a stirring picture of how human Jesus was and what He did. In them we read that Jesus:

- was the Son of Mary;

- was obedient to His parents;

- experienced hunger and thirst, sadness and happiness, anger and love.

- suffered and died.

The friends of Jesus, who traveled the same roads as He did, sharing His joys and sorrows, could not doubt that He was human—just as they were. But they came to experience and know that Jesus was more than a mere man. Jesus was divine.

Right from the first chapter of John's Gospel, we learn one of the great truths of our faith. Jesus was the **Word of God**, and the Word became flesh, taking on our human nature and dwelling among us (from John 1:14). We call this the **Incarnation**.

That Jesus was divine was expressed even more clearly by Jesus Himself when He told us about God, His Father. One day Jesus asked His followers: "Do you not believe that I am in the Father and the Father is in me?" (John 14:10). What a revelation! Here is Jesus establishing His own identity: "The Father and I are one" (John 10:30). When Jesus forgave people's sins and worked miracles— healing the sick, restoring sight to the blind, bringing the dead back to life—everyone could see that He was truly divine.

From its beginning, the Church has continually searched for a deeper understanding of Jesus. As time went on, some people forgot that Jesus was both human and divine, and disputes about Jesus arose. Some began to teach that Jesus was a great man—but only that—*a man*. Others began to teach that He was the Son of God, but denied that Jesus was fully human.

To finally answer this important question, the bishops of the Church met together in ecumenical councils and discussed the writings of the Bible, as well as the writings of learned Christian writers. With the guidance of the Holy Spirit, they proclaimed at the Council of Chalcedon in A.D. 451 this great truth of faith: Jesus Christ is true God and true man. This means that **Jesus is both human and divine**. Our Catholic faith is rooted in the whole Christ.

What do we mean by the Incarnation? What does it tell us about the humanity and divinity of Christ?

ASK: How do we know that Jesus was fully human? How do we know He is divine?

Do You Know

At Mass we express the Trinity's relationship to us in this way: "The grace of our Lord Jesus Christ and the love of God and the fellowship of the Holy Spirit be with you all." The mystery of the Blessed Trinity draws us into the very life of God. We experience that God is like an ever growing circle of love. "God is love" (1 John 4:16).

3 Jesus teaches us about God and the Kingdom of God.

Only God knows who God is. Because God was His Father, Jesus could tell His followers more about who God is and what God is really like than anyone had ever told them before. His followers knew about the one God, but Jesus was going to tell them even more about God. Jesus taught them that God is Father, Son, and Holy Spirit.

This teaching of Jesus does not mean that there are three gods. It means there are three divine Persons in one God. The **Father** is God, the **Son** is God, the **Holy Spirit** is God. And these three are one! This is what we call the **Blessed Trinity.** God is one community of three divine Persons.

Some people ask, "How can there be three Persons in one God?" This is a matter of faith. We take Jesus at His word. We reflect on this word as the Church, God's believing people. This is the teaching of the Catholic Church. This is our faith.

Jesus also taught us more about God in His teaching on the **Kingdom of God**, which is also called the Reign of God. In fact, Jesus spoke constantly about the Kingdom and wanted us to pray, "Thy Kingdom come." In this Kingdom, God's will would "be done on earth as it is in heaven."

Jesus never gave us a definition of the Kingdom of God. He used beautiful stories, called **parables**, to describe it—how important it is and how it grows. Many of these parables begin with the words "the kingdom of heaven is like." In the thirteenth chapter of Matthew's Gospel, Jesus tells us, for example, that the Kingdom can be compared to:

- a tiny, growing seed that will blossom into a great bush;
- yeast that makes bread rise;
- a buried treasure or a pearl of great price;
- a net that catches every kind of fish.

The Kingdom of God means so much. It is not a place or a political state. It is the power of God's love active in our world.

What does this mean for us? When we follow Jesus and live as His faithful followers, we help to build God's Kingdom, as Jesus showed us by His life. We are called to bring God's love to the world. This includes all people and all creation. And Jesus Himself is the Good News of God's Kingdom that is here and yet growing until the end of time.

Describe the Kingdom of God in your own words.

Prayer

Glory to the Father, and to the Son, and to the Holy Spirit. As it was in the beginning, is now, and will be forever. Amen.

Invite the young people to pray this prayer alone or to share it with their families.

Reflection and Action

Words to Remember

Find and define the following.

Incarnation The Word of God took on our human nature and "dwelt among us."

Blessed Trinity The Father, Son, and Holy Spirit—three Persons in one God.

Kingdom of God the power of God's love active in our world.

Things to Think About

Our Church has expressed beautifully the central truth of the Incarnation in this way: "By His incarnation the Son of God has united Himself in some fashion with every man. He worked with human hands, He thought with a human mind, acted by human choice, and loved with a human heart. Born of the Virgin Mary, He has truly been made one of us, like us in all things except sin."

The Church in the Modern World, 22

Things to Share

Imagine that you were one of the first followers of Jesus and were with Him every day. In your journal, write your thoughts about Jesus and His teaching about the Kingdom of God, a Kingdom of justice, peace, and love.

5 JESUS THE SAVIOR

How can we tell the difference between success and failure?

What values do you hold on to—no matter what happens? Why?

In the nineteenth century, Joseph Lister was a young English surgeon. He was eager to practice his art—to heal, to save, to make life better for his patients. But all too often he watched in anguish as surgical patients developed infections and died, after what had seemed to be a successful operation. "Why?" he asked himself. "How is it that all our medical skills can accomplish great things, yet the patient dies?"

The young surgeon searched for answers. He investigated conditions of cleanliness and patient care and found them inadequate. Later he introduced the use of a chemical spray to kill germs on surgical instruments and in the operating room. His colleagues laughed at him and resisted changing what they had always done. But Lister's work made surgery safer for all of us.

Joseph Lister stuck to his convictions, to his vision that he would make surgery safer, despite the scorn of many fellow doctors. Think now about the quality of perseverance that some people have to get things done. Then try to answer these questions.

What do you think makes a person hold on to an idea, a principle, or a project in the face of opposition?

_____

_____

_____

Do you know someone who has done this? Describe that person.

_____

_____

_____

What idea or principle would you hold on to in spite of opinions or views against you?

EXPERIENCE: Success does not mean winning approval; failure does not mean losing approval.

29

1 Jesus faithfully did the work God gave Him to do.

STRESS the underlined copy.

One of the central beliefs of the people of Old Testament times was that God would send someone to rescue them from oppression. In the time that Jesus lived on earth, there was a great deal of speculation about when this savior, or messiah, would come to Israel and what he would be like. Old Testament writers had described the Messiah as anointed king, just ruler, liberator, suffering servant, savior. He would restore Israel to its rightful place: a kingdom ruled only by God and influential over other nations.

Most of the Jewish people hoped for a powerful king who would free Israel from domination by foreigners and bring prosperity to the people. The symbol of this new kingdom was a great banquet at which the king would preside and the people of Israel would celebrate their victory over their oppressors.

Many of the people, however, were not prepared to accept Jesus as the Messiah. They were not ready for the Kingdom He would announce or the banquet He would ask them to share.

According to the Gospels, a large crowd often followed Jesus, but Jesus was never controlled by the whims of the crowd. When they wanted to make Him king, Jesus fled. When they asked Him, "Are you 'He who is to come' or do we look for another?" Jesus answered by using the words of Isaiah the prophet to describe the times of the Messiah:

> The blind can see, the lame can walk, those who suffer from dreaded skin diseases are made clean, the deaf hear, the dead are brought back to life, and the Good News is preached to the poor.
> From Matthew 11:3–5

ASK: How did Jesus contradict the prevailing ideas about what the Messiah would do?

Before the crowd could understand these words as a sign that He was the Messiah, Jesus told them, "How happy are those who have no doubts about me!" (Matthew 11:6)

Jesus did not deny that He was the Messiah, but He refused to be the kind of Messiah that the people expected. His mission was not directed toward Himself but toward His Father. The Gospels show Jesus as the Way, the Truth, and the Life. No one comes to the Father except through Jesus.

Jesus' friends realized how faithfully He had done God's will by dying to self and serving the needs of all. During His life He:

- fed the hungry and helped the poor;
- healed the sick and forgave sinners;
- told people about God and what God asked of them;
- called all people, women and men alike, to share God's life and love.

The followers of Jesus would have to obey God's will as Jesus Himself did. They would have to put aside selfishness and be His disciples. All were welcome, but it would be a hard road—one that would lead to the cross.

Why did Jesus not go along with the crowd's thinking about the Messiah?

DISCUSS some of the expectations people had for the Messiah.

2 Jesus died on the cross for us.

Jesus' determination to do His Father's will ran counter to what others wanted Him to do or to be. His disciples were no exception. One day Peter the apostle took Jesus aside and urged Him to see things differently. But Jesus was annoyed with Peter and said, "Get out of my sight! You are not judging by God's standards, but by human standards!" (from Mark 8:33).

Nothing could stop Jesus. He was completely faithful to God and to the customs and laws of His people. But He dared to interpret the Law of Moses with divine authority. Such acts brought Him into conflict with the religious and civil leaders of His time.

On the night before He died, Jesus ate His Last Supper with the disciples, celebrating the Jewish feast of Passover. Afterwards, He went out to the **Garden of Olives** with them to pray. This was a beautiful garden on a hill overlooking the city of Jerusalem. There Jesus agonized over His coming death. He prayed, "My Father, if it is possible, take this cup of suffering from me! Yet not what I want, but what you want" (Matthew 26:39).

Jesus' fear of death was very real, but His faith was rooted in His Father. He was able to face suffering and death knowing how much the Father loved Him. While Jesus prayed in the garden, He was betrayed by Judas, one of His apostles. Jesus was then arrested and brought to trial, while His other disciples left Him and ran away.

Then Jesus was brought before Pontius Pilate, the Roman governor of Judaea. Pilate asked Jesus whether He was the king of the Jews. Even though Pilate found out that Jesus was not an earthly king, he still felt that any talk of kingship not approved by Rome was a threat to Roman authority. So Pilate condemned Jesus to die.

The Roman soldiers led Jesus to the place where He would be crucified. **Crucifixion** was a form of execution used by the Romans. The cross of the common criminal was the instrument of Jesus' death. He did not struggle, protest, or resist. With trust and love, He placed His life in His Father's care: "Father! Into your hands I place my spirit!" (from Luke 23:46). Jesus said this and died. We call the day Jesus died **Good Friday**.

How did Jesus' determination to do the will of His Father affect people such as His disciples?

STRESS how important it is to respect those of different faith traditions.

Do You Know

The **Passion**, the Gospel account of Jesus' suffering and death, does not and should not allow us to blame the Jewish people of His time or our own for these events. As the Second Vatican Council teaches: "True, authorities of the Jews and those who followed their lead pressed for the death of Christ; still, what happened in His passion cannot be blamed upon all the Jews then living, without distinction, nor upon the Jews of today."

Declaration on the Relationship of the Church to Non-Christian Religions, 4

3 By rising from the dead, Jesus Christ brings us new life.

For a short time, Jesus' death destroyed the disciples' hopes that He was their Messiah. They ran and hid for fear of death or imprisonment. Then, as the Gospels record it, the unexpected happened. Some women followers of Jesus went to His burial place, expecting to anoint His body. But the large stone at the tomb's entrance had been rolled away. The tomb was empty!

The women's first thoughts were that someone had stolen the body. But they saw a young man robed in white and became frightened. "Don't be alarmed," he said. "I know you are looking for Jesus of Nazareth, who was crucified. He is not here—he has been raised! Look, here is where he was placed"(from Mark 16:6).

Word spread that Jesus was risen from the dead, but many did not know whether to believe this. The women told the apostles what they had seen and heard, but the apostles "thought that what the women said was nonsense, and they did not believe them" (Luke 24:11).

Later on the day we celebrate as **Easter Sunday**, the risen Jesus appeared to His disciples, just as He had promised. Even though they were behind locked doors, Jesus came among them and said, "Peace be with you." Jesus' disciples were filled with joy at seeing their risen Lord among them, truly risen from the dead.

Jesus had been raised up by the Father! No one was an eyewitness of the actual event. But Jesus' appearances as the Risen One convinced His disciples to have faith in the power of God. Jesus' life and death had meaning. Because of His **resurrection**, suffering and death have no final victory over us.

Through Jesus, humankind was reunited with God. The power of sin and evil was broken for all time. Through His death and resurrection, Jesus restored life to us. As Saint Paul reminds us, "For just as all people die because of their union with Adam, in the same way all will be raised to life because of their union with Christ" (1 Corinthians 15:22).

ASK: Why do you think it was so difficult for the apostles to believe that Jesus was risen?

ASSIGN for review and home study.

Church Teachings About the Savior

- Jesus died and rose again for us and for our salvation.

- The resurrection of Jesus is the central belief of our faith. We share the faith of the apostles that Jesus is risen.

- In 1 Corinthians 15:14, Paul stated the importance of the resurrection: "If Christ has not been raised from death, then we have nothing to preach and you have nothing to believe."

Prayer

Jesus Christ

is risen from the dead,

Alleluia!

DISCUSS different family customs celebrated at Easter. Read together the story of Emmaus from Luke 24:13-35.

Opposite page: Luke's account of the risen Christ with two disciples in *Supper at Emmaus,* painting by Ivo Dulčič, 1916

Reflection and Action

Words to Remember

Find and define the following.

Good Friday the day on which Jesus was crucified. _____

_____

_____

Easter Sunday the day on which Jesus Christ rose from the dead. _____

_____

Things to Think About

Jesus did the will of the Father, despite all opposition. Do you know anyone who does what he or she believes is right in spite of opposition? What happened to that person?

Do you think it takes as much or more courage today to speak about Jesus' resurrection? You may wish to write about your ideas in your journal.

Things to Share

In what ways can you live out the meaning of the life of Jesus? How will you share the hope of Christ's resurrection with others?

Encourage continued use of the prayer journal.

Unit 1 Test

A. Write each term next to the definition that matches it.

Incarnation	Inspiration
Prophets	Bible
Revelation	Blessed Trinity
Gospel	Original sin
Tradition	Old Testament
Genesis	New Testament
Messiah	Faith
	Annunciation

1. *Bible* _____ is the book that is God's word for us. It was written over many centuries by many different authors.

2. *Original sin* _____ is the first sin of humankind. It affects all human beings.

3. *Prophets* _____ were special people sent by God to speak for God and the covenant.

4. *Faith* _____ is the gift from God that helps us begin to see our lives and the world as God sees them. It is a new way of looking at life.

5. *Revelation* _____ means to make something or someone known. God tells us about God's own Self.

6. *Old Testament* _____ is the part of the Bible that tells of the relationship between God and the Israelites.

7. *Messiah* _____ means "God's anointed one," the Savior.

8. *Genesis* _____ is the name given to the first book of the Bible.

9. *Gospel* _____ is a word that means "good news." Christians use this word to describe the four accounts of Jesus' life from Matthew, Mark, Luke, and John.

10. *Blessed Trinity* _____ is the mystery of three Persons in one God, Father, Son, and Holy Spirit.

11. *Incarnation* _____ refers to the great truth of our faith: the Word of God became flesh, taking on our human nature and dwelling with us.

12. *Inspiration* _____ refers to God's special guidance under which the Bible was written.

13. *Tradition* _____ is a word that means "handed on." It refers to the truths and beliefs that have come to us from the time of Jesus and the apostles.

14. *Annunciation* _____ is the name given to the Gospel account of the angel's visit to Mary telling her that she would be the mother of the Savior.

15. *New Testament* _____ is the part of the Bible that tells about Jesus Christ, His message and mission, and His first followers.

B. Circle the response that does *not* belong.

1. We discover the answers to our questions about the meaning of life through

   a. reason.

   b. not asking questions.

   c. faith.

   d. experience.

2. This is what the Church teaches about the fall and the promise:

   a. sin entered the world through human choice.

   b. Jesus Christ fulfills God's promise to free human beings to share in God's life.

   c. every human being suffers the effects of original sin.

   (d.) God trapped Adam and Eve into committing sin.

3. The story of creation in Genesis' teaches that

   (a.) the world must have been created in seven 24-hour days.

   b. God alone created everything that is.

   c. the world God created is good.

   d. God is all-powerful, all-loving, all-good.

4. The Gospel accounts in the Bible tell us

   (a.) the complete biography of Jesus' life.

   b. that Jesus was the Son of Mary.

   c. that Jesus was truly human.

   d. that Jesus was divine.

5. The Gospel tells us that

   a. Jesus died for us on Good Friday.

   b. Jesus did the will of the Father always.

   (c.) the apostles immediately believed the women's story of the resurrection.

   d. Jesus appeared to his followers on Easter Sunday.

C. **Respond as thoughtfully and completely as possible.**

1. Is faith easy for you, or difficult? Explain. How can your faith be strengthened?

   (Encourage the young people to reflect seriously before

   responding.)

   _____

   _____

2. What part can you play in working and caring for creation?

   (Accept appropriate responses.)

   _____

   _____

   _____

3. Can you explain the meaning of these symbols from the story of Adam and Eve?

   the garden: Symbol of happiness and of God's grace—

   our sharing in God's life.

   the serpent: Symbol of evil present in the world.

   _____

   being sent from the garden: Symbol of turning away

   from God; loss of grace.

4. What does the "Kingdom of God" mean to you? Does it affect your life? How?

   (There are no incorrect answers here, but encourage serious

   thought.)

   _____

   _____

5. When Jesus died on the cross, many considered Him to be a failure. What do you think about that? How might the example of Jesus help you to cope with failure?

   (Accept all answers. Help the young people to begin to see

   success/failure in terms of faith.)

   _____

   _____

6 JESUS SENDS THE HOLY SPIRIT

Who helps us to be sure that everything we believe about God is true?

Where do we get the courage and hope we need to face the challenges in our lives?

Elena's assignment was to write about the sounds and sights of early morning in spring. This is what she wrote:

"The first spring morning is here at last! The sun has come back, burning brightly. Everywhere, I hear the sound of birds! The air is filled with their glad songs welcoming the season of new life!"

Here is a very different description of a spring morning:

"Over increasingly large areas of the United States, spring now comes unheralded by the return of the birds, and the early mornings are strangely silent where once they were filled with the beauty of bird songs."

The writer was Rachel Carson. In a book called *Silent Spring,* she told why our springs are becoming silent. She said we are killing off our birds with poisonous chemicals.

Rachel Carson's words were believed by some people; laughed at by others. But she went right on warning us about the terrible things we are doing to our world. The spirit of Rachel Carson is reflected today in the intense concern we feel for our environment.

How has this spirit made your community more conscious of protecting the environment?

_____

_____

Among any group of people, why is spirit such an important factor?

_____

_____

EXPERIENCE: We sense the importance of *spirit* as a force which binds us together increasing our awareness of the world around us.

1 Jesus promised to send His disciples the Holy Spirit as their Helper.

We all need visions, goals, and some type of spirit to hold us together. We need courage and hope and someone to guide us. These Jesus has given to us in a way we never could have imagined.

On the night before He died, Jesus promised to stay with His apostles always. He would send the Holy Spirit to help, guide, and encourage them. The Holy Spirit would help them find the way to live and bring Jesus' message of God's love to all the world.

Jesus told His friends some of the things the Holy Spirit would do for them. The Spirit would:

- remain with them and in them;
- teach them and help them remember all that Jesus said;
- lead them to the truth;
- give them the strength to be His witnesses.

From John 14—16

The **Holy Spirit** is the Third Person of the Blessed Trinity. This same Spirit guides and strengthens us today as members of God's family. At all times, the Spirit is in us and with us. The Spirit draws us together as God's people, making us one in truth and love.

When you feel in need of help, do you ever ask the Holy Spirit to help you?

ASK: What signs of the Holy Spirit do you see in our world?

Do You Know

Jesus called the Holy Spirit the Paraclete, a word with many meanings. Paraclete means helper, friend, consoler, teacher, guide, and defender—as Jesus Christ is to us. Because the Spirit is invisible, like the wind, we know the unseen Spirit only by what the Spirit does to and for us in the Church.

2 **The Holy Spirit came at Pentecost.**

After Jesus ascended to the Father in heaven, the apostles went back to Jerusalem. There they often came together to pray. We read the New Testament account of how, in an earthshaking scene, the Holy Spirit came upon them.

> When the day of Pentecost came, all the believers were gathered together in one place. Suddenly there was a noise from the sky which sounded like a strong wind blowing, and it filled the whole house where they were sitting. Then they saw what looked like tongues of fire which spread out and touched each person there. They were all filled with the Holy Spirit and began to talk in other languages, as the Spirit enabled them to speak.
> Acts 2:1–4

Here was the Holy Spirit at work through people. As a result:

- thousands of people changed their lives and were baptized;

- their sins were forgiven;

DISCUSS: What happened as a result of the coming of the Holy Spirit?

- they, too, shared in the gift of the Holy Spirit;

- the Holy Spirit made them one in their love for God and one another.

We read in Acts 2:42–47 how the early Christians lived. They shared their possessions in common, they cared for the needy, and they lived in fellowship and prayer. This is how the Holy Spirit made them one in love for God and one another.

Name one way you can show that you are a genuine Christian.

NOTE: Have the group read the full account in Acts 2:42-47.

NOTE: The day on which the Holy Spirit came upon the apostles is called Pentecost—50 days after Easter.

3 The Holy Spirit helped the disciples be Christ's witnesses.

The Holy Spirit would truly guide the community of Jesus' **disciples**. At first they were a timid and fearful group who had run away when Jesus was arrested, tried, and put to death. With the help of the Spirit, however, they became strong and fearless. The Holy Spirit filled them with the fire of faith and the courage to proclaim what they knew was true.

The apostle Peter declared to the crowds that filled Jerusalem on **Pentecost**, fifty days after Easter:

Jesus of Nazareth was a man whose divine authority was clearly proven to you by all the miracles and wonders which God performed through him. God has raised this very Jesus from death, and we are all witnesses to this fact. Jesus has been raised to the right side of God, his Father, and has received from the Father the Holy Spirit, as the Father had promised. What you now see and hear is the gift that Jesus has poured out on us.
From Acts 2:22, 32–33

Then Peter concluded, "All the people of Israel are to know for sure that this Jesus is the one

that God has made Lord and Messiah!" (from Acts 2:36).

The community of Jesus' disciples was called to share this message that Peter proclaimed. They would be Jesus' witnesses in the world. The Holy Spirit helped them to remember what Jesus had said:

Go, then, to all peoples everywhere and make them my disciples: baptize them in the name of the Father, the Son, and the Holy Spirit, and teach them to obey everything I have commanded you. And I will be with you always, to the end of the age.
Matthew 28:19–20

The Spirit of Jesus would dwell in their hearts, making them one with Him and with one another. Together they would form His Church. Today the Holy Spirit continues to guide us. It is this same Spirit who is with us as we try to live as followers of Jesus Christ.

In our next chapter we will learn more about the Church.

How did the Holy Spirit help the first followers of Christ?

Why do we, as followers of Christ, need the guidance of the Holy Spirit today?

40

Church Teachings About the Holy Spirit

● Jesus Christ sent His disciples the gift of the Holy Spirit.

● The Holy Spirit is the Third Person of the Blessed Trinity.

● The Holy Spirit is the source of life, unity, and truth in the Church.

● The Holy Spirit is the Paraclete: helper, consoler, teacher, and guide.

Prayer

Leader: Come, Holy Spirit,
fill the hearts of Your faithful,
and kindle in them
the fire of Your love.

All: Send forth Your Spirit
and they shall be created.
And You shall renew the face
of the earth.

Leader: Let us pray.

All: O God, by the light of the Holy Spirit You have taught the hearts of Your faithful. In the Holy Spirit help us to know what is right and to rejoice in Your love. We ask this through Christ our Lord. Amen

NOTE: Invite the group to share this prayer together.

Reflection and Action

Words to Remember

Find and define the following.

disciples followers of Jesus Christ.
_____
_____

Holy Spirit the Third Person of the Blessed Trinity; the Paraclete.
_____
_____

Pentecost the day on which the Holy Spirit came upon the disciples, 50 days after Easter.
_____
_____

Things to Think About

Jesus told us many things about the Holy Spirit. How do you prefer to think of the Holy Spirit? As a Helper? Teacher? Consoler? Defender? Why?

Do you believe that the Holy Spirit can do for you what was done for the apostles and first disciples? How could the Spirit help you right now in your life?

Things to Share

The very thought of God is and should be awesome for us. But even more awesome is that God is so active in our world and in our lives. Do you realize how important the Holy Spirit is in your life? Share your thoughts with someone you trust or put them into your own words in a prayer to the Holy Spirit.

7 THE CATHOLIC CHURCH

To what groups do you belong?

What identity do you share with them?

Every group to which we belong—a family, a team, a school or a parish—has its own identity.

Some signs of identity are easy to spot. For example, you can tell school sports teams by the color of their uniforms.

Listed below are identifying qualities that might help others recognize a certain family, school, or parish.

Choose one of these three groups: a family, a school, or a parish. Then select four identifying qualities or traits by which others can recognize the group.

I.D. Qualities

We care about fairness.

We share a common name.

We believe in God.

We work for peace.

We share meals.

We have the same ancestors.

We pray.

We share good times together.

We welcome others.

We _____

Show your I.D. qualities to one other person. Then share and compare your choices.

Suppose that you have a new friend who is not a member of the Catholic Church. He or she wonders what Catholics are like and what they believe.

Before you answer, it might help to ask yourself:

What does it mean for me to be a Catholic?

How do I show others that I am a member of the Church?

What might I tell my friend about what Catholics believe?

What qualities do you think identify the Church?

1 Jesus invites us to follow Him in His Church.

STRESS the underlined copy.

Jesus is the One who gives us our identity as a people and as individuals. From the very beginning of His life work, Jesus called people to follow Him. He said, "Come follow me!" People listened to His message. They heard His promise of a new way of life.

When people were sick in body and soul, Jesus healed them and forgave them. He helped them feel more positive about themselves. He made everyone feel like somebody. Jesus wanted people to take an interest in one another. He fulfilled their need to belong.

ASK: What "mission" did the apostles have?

As more and more people responded to Jesus' invitation to follow Him, they spent time together. Jesus shared with them His teachings and His way of life. Among His disciples were twelve special followers. Later on they would be called the **apostles**, a word meaning "those sent on a mission."

The apostles were twelve disciples whom Jesus chose for a special role in His community. They were a close-knit group of friends. They stayed with Jesus and traveled together. They got to know Jesus and one another.

Jesus held the apostles together as a group. With them Jesus formed the community we call **Church**. This is the special name for those who call themselves Christians and follow the way of Jesus, rooted in beliefs and traditions that go back through the centuries to the apostles.

ASK: Has anyone or any group offered you an invitation to belong? How did this make you feel?

As members of the Church, the source of our identity is Christ, but we are energized by the Holy Spirit. The Spirit:

- makes us one;
- calls us to worship and pray;
- guides the Church in teaching, serving, and governing.

Our faith community is reminded of this at the Sunday celebration of the Eucharist when we pray the ancient Profession of Faith. We proclaim together, "We believe in one, holy, catholic, and apostolic Church." This is our belief, and it is a good description of the Church. As Catholics we pray to make it true in our lives.

One, **holy**, **catholic**, **apostolic**—these are the four identifying **marks**, or qualities, of the Church founded by Jesus Christ. Through them the Church is known and recognized. These four marks of the Church are both gifts of God and challenges to us. We can think of them as:

- seeds to cultivate;
- talents to develop;
- ideals to strive for.

What does the word *apostle* mean?

What are the four identifying marks of the Church?

Sermon on the Mount by Fra Angelico (*c.* 1400–1455)

44

2 The Church is one and holy.

At the Last Supper, Jesus prayed to His Father for His followers "that they may be one just as you and I are one" (John 17:11). Saint Paul also spoke of the Christian community as one. He spoke of the Church in terms of the body. The body has a marvelous unity. Each part has its own function, and all parts work for the good of the whole body.

Saint Paul wrote, "All of you are Christ's body, and each one is a part of it" (1 Corinthians 12:27). **Oneness**, then, is a special mark by which we identify the Church and its members. Together we form the one body of Christ.

The New Testament letter to the Ephesians lists some of the signs and causes of our unity, the things that make us **one**:

- there is one body and one Spirit;
- we have one hope to which God has called us;
- we accept one Lord, one faith, one Baptism.

From Ephesians 4:4–5

NOTE: You might want to have the group read more of Ephesians 4:1-16.

Do You Know

The Church founded on Jesus Christ and guided by the Holy Spirit must develop, change, and grow through the centuries. But it must always be Christ's one Church. Jesus left no detailed blueprint as to how His Church should look, how it would celebrate, in what variety of works it would engage. But it would be His one Church nonetheless. He breathed His Spirit upon His apostles. He sent His Spirit into the hearts of believers to be ever with the Church, guiding it to truth and unity. These believers truly were, and are today, the Church.

As Catholic Christians we celebrate our unity in the Eucharist. As a community we are nourished by the Body and Blood of Christ and strengthened in our one common faith. We also celebrate the other sacraments and have as our leaders the bishops, with the Pope as their head. The Church, then, is one.

Holiness is another mark by which we identify the Church. We are called to carry out in our lives our loving relationship with God and with one another. We do this through lives of prayer, especially the celebration of the sacraments, and by serving others.

By His death and resurrection, Jesus prepared the way for people to become more holy. He called us to be a holy people dedicated to God, the Holy One, and dedicated to one another. In a word, Jesus says, "You must be perfect—just as your Father in heaven is perfect" (Matthew 5:48).

Being **holy** is not something people are born with. Only God is holy. Our holiness is always a share in God's holiness. Holiness is the mark of those who listen to the Gospel message and respond to it.

Jesus gives new life in Baptism. He expressed this by saying, "I have come in order that you might have life—life in all its fullness" (John 10:10). Only by trying consciously to do what is right can we begin to grow in holiness. Our daily challenge is to live as Jesus taught.

How eagerly the first Christians accepted the challenge of living a life of faith and good works! By word and example they showed forth what they believed. They were one in mind and heart, sharing with one another everything they owned and giving witness to the resurrection of the Lord Jesus.

Then, and now, holiness is one of the chief identifying marks of the Church. Throughout the ages our Church has guided many to lead holy lives.

What are some signs that the Church is one? holy?

What can you do as a Catholic to show forth the unity and holiness of the Church by the way you live?

3 The Church is catholic (universal) and apostolic.

The Church of Jesus Christ is not to be something exclusive, a closed community. It is supposed to be open to everyone. Jesus came not just for a certain group, but for all people. So Jesus sent His apostles to reach as many people as possible.

This openness to people of all nations is one of His Church's essential identifying marks. The Church is to include people of every race, color, and nationality. The rich and the poor, the wanted and the unwanted—all are equally welcomed to hear the Good News of salvation. The Church is to be **catholic**, that is, universal and worldwide.

Jesus' salvation is for all. So is His Church. "The Son of Man came to seek and to save the lost" (Luke 19:10). In fact, we see that the Church is everywhere, all over the world—in all cultures and using all languages.

Jesus entrusted His Church to leaders whom He had formed in faith. He had confidence in His apostles. He told them that the Holy Spirit would always be with them. The Spirit would help them preach the Good News to the whole world.

The Church would grow and build on the faith of the apostles. The Church would be **apostolic.** Jesus told His apostles, "Go to all peoples everywhere and make them my disciples. And I will be with you always, to the end of the age."
From Matthew 28:19–20

With the coming of the Holy Spirit on Pentecost, the Church burst forth into the world. Jesus had handed over the roles of leadership and service in His community to Peter and the other apostles. This community was sent by Jesus to preach the Good News and to witness to His presence with them. The Church was then, as it is now, the visible sign of Christ's continuing work in the world.

Catholic believers hold that the Church was founded on Christ with Peter and the apostles as its first leaders and teachers. Their authority

and call to service has been handed down to their successors, the Pope and bishops of the Catholic Church. This is why the Catholic Church is apostolic.

Besides the Catholic Church there are other Christian communities in the world. As Catholics we respect them and recognize Christ working in them. With them we pray that Jesus' prayer for unity among all who believe in Him may be realized.

All Christian churches are not the same, however. As Catholics, we believe that the fullness of Christ's action and the working of the Holy Spirit is with the Catholic Church. To deny our belief would betray the work of the Holy Spirit.

What are some practical and positive ways in which you can act to promote the goal of unity among all Christians?

Church Teachings About the Church

- The Church is one, holy, catholic (universal), and apostolic. By these four marks the Church of Jesus Christ is known and recognized.

- The Holy Spirit guides and preserves the Church in its true identity as the faith community founded by Christ.

- Christ is the cornerstone of the Church.

- Peter and the apostles were the first leaders of the Church. The apostolic authority and call to service is handed down to their successors: the Pope and bishops of the Catholic Church.

Prayer

Leader: We pray for the Church that we may continue to be a sign of openness and welcome for all who seek fellowship and justice.

All: Lord, hear our prayer.

Leader: We pray for the Church that we may continue to live in the spirit of the apostles, faithful to Your Word and dedicated to Your work.

All: Lord, hear our prayer.

ASK: What more can we do to promote unity among Christians?

Reflection and Action

Words to Remember

Find and define the following.

one The Church is one because there is one Lord, one faith, one Baptism.

holy The Church is holy because we share God's life through the sacraments.

catholic The Church is catholic because it is worldwide, universal.

apostolic The Church is apostolic because it was founded on Christ with Peter and the apostles as its first leaders.

Things to Think About

The four marks of the Church are both identifying qualities and challenges to its members. They challenge us to **oneness** and **holiness** in a **universal** Church that works to fulfill the **apostolic** mission to bring Christ to all people and all people to Christ.

How do I show the members of the Church that I care about them?

Things to Share

Imagine that a trusted friend asked you: "Have you ever experienced the love of Christ for you in the Church?" How would you respond? Then ask yourself: Has anyone ever felt the love of Christ in something I did? When and where was it? Write down your thoughts in your prayer journal.

8 THE SEVEN SACRAMENTS

How do you know someone loves you?

How do you show others that you love them?

Thea Bowman grew up in a small southern town where her family, sadly, like so many African-American families, was a victim of racism. But the love of God was so strong in Thea's heart that she did not become bitter or seek revenge.

When she was only fifteen, Thea joined the Franciscan Sisters of Perpetual Adoration. Soon her many gifts as a gospel singer, teacher, and artist blossomed like cherry trees in the spring.

Sister Thea Bowman put all of her energy into serving Jesus and His Church. She was determined to help the Church appreciate and accept African-American music and culture. With humor and song, she broke down the walls between people. Sister Thea became a sign of healing.

When she told gospel stories and challenged people to live up to Jesus' vision of justice and peace, people listened. Her powerful message inspired children, parents, teachers, and even bishops. Sister Thea was a sign of life for everyone.

She had a vision of unity for all in the Church. This is how she described it: "If we work together, play together, stand together, pray together, then we can create a new heaven."

In 1990 Sister Thea died of bone cancer. But she still lives on in the Church she loved, as a radiant sign of healing, life, and love.

Is there someone in your life who is a sign of healing? Of life? Of love?

In what way do you think Sister Thea was most like Christ?

What are some signs that Jesus Christ is with us in the Church today?

EXPERIENCE: In a very real way we are each called to live *sacramental* lives—to be signs of Christ's presence in our world.

STRESS the underlined copy.

1 Jesus used signs to show his love and power.

God's chosen family in the Old Testament lived by signs, signs that showed how God was acting among His people and shaping their lives. People interpreted even the ordinary things that happened as signs that God was taking care of their needs. The rain, the light and warmth of the sun, a family, a long life, and a homeland signified God's care for them.

God's care for people was never one-sided. God always met both their physical and spiritual needs. In the great Exodus event, God led the Israelite people out of slavery in Egypt to become a free people. When they cried for help and food, God provided manna, "bread from heaven." This was a sign to the Chosen People that they could always depend on God because God was always with them.

A sign can be contained in a person, an event, or in the traditions of a community. Through their words and deeds, the prophets were signs of God's concern for the people. The many times God rescued Israel from destruction or defeat were all signs of God's love for them.

In His life and teaching, Jesus made it clear to us that He is as concerned about our needs as we are. In our everyday experiences, Jesus urges us to look for the signs of God's love and care for us. Jesus said to His disciples, "Look how the wild flowers grow: they do not work or make clothes for themselves. But I tell you that not even King Solomon with all his wealth had clothes as beautiful as one of these flowers" (Luke 12:27).

Jesus Himself is the greatest sign and gift of God's love. In His dealings with people, Jesus always showed God's love. Like a parent bending to comfort or feed a child or to soothe a family's fears, Jesus was there caring for people in need.

Ask: How did Jesus "show" us God?

Jesus met the blind, the deaf, the lame, the sick—and healed them. He saved them, doing for them what they could not do for themselves. He fed the hungry, taught the ignorant, found the lost, and brought them back to God's love and friendship. The Gospels describe how Jesus did this.

These and other signs of God's love Jesus shared and entrusted with those who came after Him, as we shall see.

Why do we say that Jesus is the greatest sign of God's love?   (See second paragraph above.)

How did Jesus show God's love and power?

(See third paragraph above.)

In the Gospels, Jesus teaches the members of His Church that concern for others is a very important part of being His disciple. From the beginning, the Church has been an example of service and caring for those in need. The Church carries out the mission of service in many ways and at all levels. There are many international agencies of the Church that work to alleviate hunger, poverty, and disease all over the world. The Church in each nation is also dedicated to meeting the particular needs of people, whether they be physical, economic, educational or spiritual.

From experience you may be aware of the work people in your parish are doing to serve your community. Participation in works of service is the responsibility of every Catholic.

How is the Church a sign of God's love in the world?   It continues what Jesus began.

How can you be a sign of God's love in our world?   (stress prayer and service)

NOTE: You may wish to review the sacraments chart on page 116.

2 The Church is a sign of God's life and love among us.

After Pentecost, the apostles and first Christians set about the task of spreading the Good News of Jesus Christ. This active community was the early Church as Jesus had founded it. Since that time, men and women of faith have sought to establish the Church in every nation throughout the world.

By proclaiming and living out the Gospel message, the Church continues what Jesus began. The Church, therefore, is a sign of God's life and love among us. It is also the means through which God shares the divine life and love with us. In the community of the Church, we meet Christ, especially when we pray and worship together. In living by His example and by following His teaching, we become signs of Christ. In what practical ways can we do this?

Do You Know

Whenever the Pope and the bishops, the successors of the apostles, come together as an ecumenical council to speak and teach in Jesus' name, the Spirit is with them guiding them in truth. When councils solemnly define doctrinal beliefs, the Holy Spirit guides the bishops on teaching the truth. We speak of this gift in the Church as *infallibility*. We believe that the Pope has this same gift when he specifically defines doctrinal beliefs as official Catholic teachings.

3 The seven sacraments are life-giving signs.

Among the ways the Church is a sign of God's love and care are particular acts of worship or community celebrations we call **sacraments**. Sacraments are effective signs of Jesus' presence in our community. There are seven sacraments. They cause to happen what they signify. Each sacrament marks a particular time of growth as a Christian and invites us to share in God's life in a special way.

The Church invites us to full participation in Christ's life through the Sacraments of Initiation: Baptism, Confirmation and Eucharist. Through these three sacraments, we are welcomed into the Church, strengthened in faith by the Holy Spirit, and nourished by Christ Himself.

To be baptized means a new birth, a sharing in new life. Baptism is the first sacrament of our initiation into the Church. Through Baptism, the life and love of God, which we call **grace**, is given to us and we are freed from original sin. To confirm Christians in this new life, Jesus sent the Holy Spirit. The Church celebrates this event on Pentecost and at every Confirmation. Finally, through the Eucharist we complete our initiation into the Church. For the rest of our lives, we will be sustained and nourished by this sacrament of Jesus' Body and Blood.

Two other sacraments, Reconciliation and Anointing of the Sick, are known as the Sacraments of Healing. In the celebration of the sacrament of Reconciliation, the Church experiences God's loving forgiveness. Those who sin and are sorry for sin turn back to God and are forgiven. They are reunited with God and reconciled with their brothers and sisters in the Church.

NOTE: The sacraments fulfill our human needs through initiation and nourishment, healing and forgiveness, love and service.

The sacrament of the Anointing of the Sick calls upon the whole Church to care for sick or aged members. When members of the Church are seriously ill, the Church prays that they may be healed and that their faith may be strengthened.

Finally, we have two Sacraments of Service. In Matrimony we celebrate the union of a man and a woman. The community is a witness to their vows to love each other as Christ loves His Church.

In Holy Orders we celebrate the ordaining of bishops, priests, and deacons to serve as God's ministers to the Christian community. Those ordained promise to serve all the needs of the community.

The sacraments are truly sources of life for us. In them, the faith-filled community of the Church meets the risen Christ.

How is the Church a sign of Christ?

Through the love and care expressed in the sacraments.

Church Teachings About the Sacraments

- Jesus Christ is the sacrament of God: the most perfect sign of the invisible God. In Him we meet the invisible God in a visible way: we can see, hear, and touch God.

- The Church is the sacrament of Christ, the visible sign by which we meet, touch, and are touched by Christ.

- The seven sacraments are effective signs of what happens within us by the power of God and actions of Christ through His Church.

- The sacraments help us to grow in holiness, build up the Body of Christ, and give worship to God.

Prayer

Almighty and eternal God,
You have blessed all creation with signs
of Your love and power,
especially through Your Son
and the Church He founded.
We thank You now and in all our days.
Through Christ our Lord. Amen.

Reflection and Action

Words to Remember

Find and define the following.

sign a person, event, or the traditions of a community that reveal God to us.

sacrament an effective sign of Jesus' presence in our community; sacraments cause to happen what they signify.

Things to Think About

God, who is invisible to us, is revealed to us through people and through things. So it is not surprising that in the sacraments we begin with things we can see, feel, or hear: water, oil, bread and wine, human words and gestures. All of these are a part of the celebration of the sacraments, in which Christ is truly present with us.

Do you ever thank Jesus for His gift of the sacraments to us? You may want to write a prayer of thanksgiving in your journal.

Things to Share

Sacraments are not private celebrations. They are celebrations of the Christian community that assembles to hear the word of God and to experience Christ's presence in a unique and special way. See whether you can explain to someone in your own words how Jesus acts in and through the sacraments.

9 BECOMING CATHOLIC

How good is your imagination?

Can you picture what your Baptism was like?

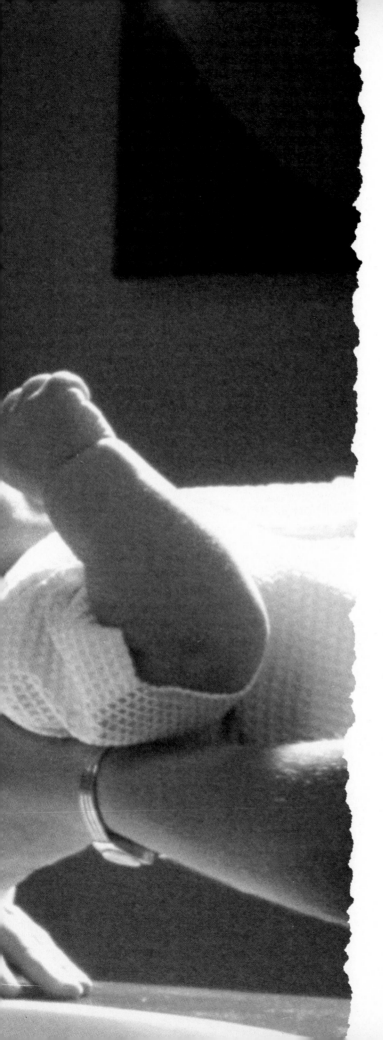

Your mother or father has dressed you all in white for a very special day.

Your parents and two other people who keep kissing you on your bald head are sitting in the front pew. You are in a beautiful church that is filled with people and music.

A man who is also dressed in white greets your family by name. He smiles and says a word that you will hear over and over today. That word is "Welcome!"

Then you feel some water flowing over your head, and your heart pounds a little faster.

The man in white holds you up in his arms for everyone to see. He calls out your name.

All of a sudden everyone is clapping and smiling at you as if you were their own child.

What has happened?

Why is that word "Welcome!" so important on this day?

EXPERIENCE: Explain that our "decision" to become Catholic begins at our Baptism. It was made for us by our family (if we were infants), but later we must consciously renew our Baptism and our commitment to Christ.

1 In the sacrament of Baptism we are welcomed into the Church.

STRESS the underlined copy

At the end of the Gospel of Matthew Jesus tells His first disciples, "Go to all peoples everywhere and make them my disciples: baptize them in the name of the Father, the Son, and the Holy Spirit" (from Matthew 28:19). These words show us some very important things about the Church and our life in the Church:

- the Church is open to all people everywhere—all are invited to be one with Christ;

- we begin our life in the Church through the sacrament of Baptism; we share this sacrament with every member of the Church;

- one important part of Baptism is being welcomed: all nations, races, ages, people well known or unknown, rich or poor, are welcome in the Church.

Each of us in the Church shares this welcome and is called to share it with others. In a world where it is common to leave some people out, to cut them off or hold them back and to favor others, it is good to find that the Church tries to welcome all without distinction. This, after all, is what Jesus did.

Many kinds of people followed Jesus, seeking to hear His message and share in His life. But sometimes people tried to keep others away from Him. These people thought that sinners, the poor, and the sick might be the "wrong kind" of people to be in Jesus' company. Jesus, however, insisted that it was *especially* for these people, the lost sheep who needed His love and care, that He had come.

Even His disciples could misunderstand what Jesus intended. One time they scolded people who brought their children for Jesus to bless. But Jesus welcomed the children, took them in His arms, and blessed them.

We, too, are welcomed when we come to the community of the Church. In fact, some of the first words we hear from the priest or deacon at Baptism are words of welcome.

These words are a part of our initiation into the Church. We call the process of becoming a member of the Church **Christian initiation**. We are **initiated** into the Church through the sacraments of Baptism, Confirmation, and Eucharist. These sacraments are celebrated in our parish, which welcomes us and also cares for us.

In Baptism we are called by name to begin a lifelong relationship with God in the Church. **Baptism** is the first and basic sacrament. Through Baptism:

- we receive the Holy Spirit;

- we are reborn as children of God and our sins are forgiven;

- we become members of the Church;

- we begin our journey in faith, filled with God's life, presence, and favor. It is a journey that will continue all our lives.

If we were baptized as babies, our parents and godparents affirmed their own faith and promised to help us grow as faithful Christians.

Do you know anyone, a young person or an adult, who is preparing to become a Catholic? If you do, ask that person what becoming a part of the Church means to him or her.

What are the names of your godparents? Why not speak to them about your Baptism and thank them for what they have done for you and for your faith?

DISCUSS: Why do you think that eventually the decision to belong to the Church must be our very own?

2 Baptism frees us from sin and gives us God's life of grace.

NOTE: Read the whole account in John 3:1–13.

Jesus has told us even more about the meaning of our Baptism. One day a man named Nicodemus was speaking with Jesus about the Kingdom of God. Jesus told him, "No one can enter the Kingdom of God unless that person is born of water and the Holy Spirit" (from John 3:5).

Why do you think Jesus talked about being "born of water"? Think for a moment about the precious gift of water. Without water we could not live. Water makes things grow and cleanses things, making them bright and new.

In the Bible, water is also used as a symbol of life and growth and cleansing. Think how God's people in the Old Testament passed through the waters of the Red Sea, from slavery to freedom, from death to new life. You may wish to read the story of this wonderful event in Exodus 14:1—15:27.

NOTE: Read it now.

Now in Baptism the Spirit of Jesus is poured out on us. The Spirit not only gives new life and rebirth, but also cleanses and makes us new. The very word baptize means "to wash clean."

Through the waters of Baptism, we share in Christ's death and resurrection. We rise with Him to new life through this sacrament.

Baptism also breaks our ties to sin. All of us have been born into this world with **original sin**. Through Baptism we are freed from this sin. However, we need to overcome the effects of this sin as well as we can. Even though we have a tendency to sin, we can choose to do what is right as baptized followers of Christ. With God's grace and the help and support of our family and parish, we can do this.

Through Baptism we become children of God, sharers of God's own life, and brothers and sisters of Christ in our community of faith.

What does Baptism do for us?

What can you do today to show your gratitude for the gift of Baptism?

Share together about the many beautiful symbols used in the rite of Baptism, e.g. water, holy oil, white garment, candle.

Do You Know

The ordinary minister of Baptism is a bishop, priest, or deacon. But in an emergency, any person with the right intention can baptize. This is done by pouring water on the person's forehead and saying the words that are always used in the sacrament of Baptism: "I baptize you in the name of the Father, and of the Son, and of the Holy Spirit."

57

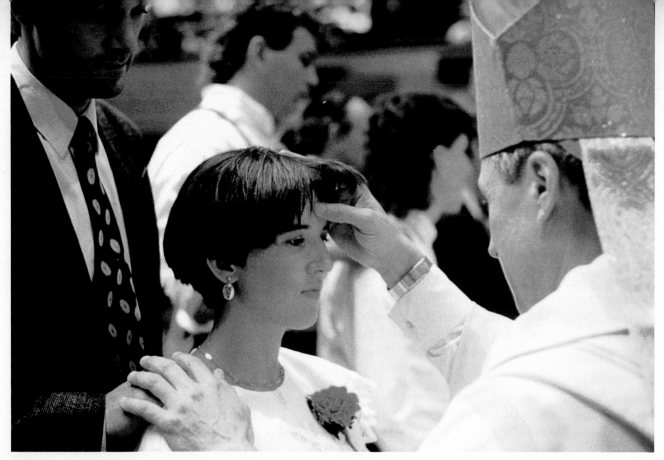

DISCUSS how Confirmation strengthens our personal decision to be a Catholic.

3 Confirmation strengthens us to be witnesses to our faith.

The sacrament of Confirmation is another step in becoming fully initiated members of the Church. Confirmation is very closely related to Baptism.

When we celebrate the sacrament of **Confirmation**, we experience, affirm, and receive in a deeper way the life of the Holy Spirit that we first received in Baptism. This is the Spirit of truth whom Jesus promised to send and who would guide us always.

In Confirmation the persons being confirmed are anointed with holy oil as a sign of being sealed, or confirmed, with the Holy Spirit. During the rite, the bishop says to each, "(Name), be sealed with the Gift of the Holy Spirit." The person responds, "Amen." The confirmed Catholics are now called upon to be Spirit-filled witnesses to God's love and Jesus' message of justice and peace.

When we are confirmed, the Holy Spirit strengthens us with special gifts

- to help us live as faithful followers and true witnesses of Jesus Christ;
- to strengthen our minds and our wills to do what Christ asks of us.

The gifts of the Holy Spirit are:

STRESS: It is up to each person to *use* these gifts. They are not automatic.

- wisdom and understanding;
- right judgment and courage;
- knowledge and reverence;
- wonder and awe in God's presence.

Baptism and Confirmation are two Sacraments of Initiation. We receive them only once. They are special moments on the journey of faith.

In the next two chapters we will learn about the third Sacrament of Initiation, the Eucharist. As we shall see, it is this sacrament that will nourish us frequently for the rest of our lives.

What can confirmed Catholics do to show they are followers of Jesus Christ?

Which gift of the Holy Spirit do you feel most in need of at this time of your life?

Church Teachings: Baptism and Confirmation

- Baptism and Confirmation are two of the three Sacraments of Initiation. (The other is the Eucharist.)

- Baptism is the first and necessary sacrament that celebrates our rebirth into new life.

- Through Baptism we become members of the Body of Christ, the Church. We are set free from sin and share in the life of God through grace.

- In Confirmation we are sealed with the Gift of the Holy Spirit and strengthened to live as faithful followers of Christ.

Prayer

O God, in Baptism we are welcomed into the Church. In Confirmation we are strengthened with Your Holy Spirit. Help us to be true witnesses to You, living lives of faith, hope, and love. We ask this through Jesus Christ, Your Son, Our Lord. Amen.

Reflection and Action

Words to Remember

Find and define the following.

Baptism The sacrament through which we receive the Holy Spirit, are reborn as God's children, are forgiven, and become members of the Church.

Confirmation The sacrament through which we experience, affirm, and receive, in a deeper way, the gift of the Holy Spirit.

Things to Think About

At the door of the church there is a font containing holy water. When we enter the church, we put our fingers into the holy water and then make the sign of the cross. This action reminds us of the waters of Baptism.

The next time you enter your parish church and bless yourself with holy water, use that moment to recall your own Baptism and the promises made to reject sin and profess faith.

STRESS that holy water is a sacramental that helps us to remember Baptism.

Things to Share

Share with God your feelings of gratitude for the gifts of Baptism and Confirmation. Talk over with God ways you might bring the presence of Christ more clearly and meaningfully into your life in your family and your parish.

Unit 2 Test

A. Write each term next to the definition that matches it.

Confirmation   Pentecost

Grace   Apostle

Baptism   Disciples

Christian Initiation   Holy Spirit

Holy   One

Apostolic   Catholic

Sacraments of Initiation Infallibility

Church

1. _Holy Spirit_ _____ is the third Person of the Blessed Trinity who guides and strengthens the Church.

2. _Grace_ _____ is the life and love of God that fills our lives.

3. _Disciple_ _____ is the name given to those who follow the teachings of Jesus.

4. _Pentecost_ _____ is the day on which the Holy Spirit came upon the followers of Jesus.

5. _One_ _____ is the mark that describes the unity of the Church.

6. _Church_ _____ is the community of believers who follow the teachings of Jesus Christ.

7. _Baptism_ _____ is the sacrament through which we are reborn as children of God and become members of the Church.

8. _Apostle_ _____ is the name that means "sent on a mission." The name was given to those chosen by Jesus to help them begin the Church.

9. _Holy_ _____ is a mark that identifies the Church as a community of those who follow Christ in prayer and service.

10. _Christian Initiation_ _____ is the process by which we become members of the Church.

11. _Confirmation_ _____ is the sacrament through which we affirm and receive in a deeper way the life of the Spirit given us in Baptism.

12. _Infallibility_ _____ means that the Pope and bishops are guided in truth when defining doctrines of faith and morals.

13. _Catholic_ _____ is a mark of the Church that identifies it as universal, open to all who believe.

14. _Sacraments of Initiation_ _____ is a name given to the sacraments of Baptism, Confirmation, and Eucharist.

15. _Apostolic_ _____ is the mark that identifies the Church as founded on Christ with Peter and the apostles as its first leaders and teachers.

B. Circle the response that does *not* belong.

1. Jesus told His followers that the Holy Spirit would

   a. remain with them forever.

   b. come to them on Palm Sunday.

   c. lead them to the truth.

   d. strengthen them to be His witnesses.

2. The marks of the Church identify it as

   a. an exclusive closed community.

   b. a community dedicated to God and one another.

   c. based on apostolic authority.

   d. welcoming to all people.

60

3. The sacraments are

    a. life-giving signs of Christ's presence.

    b. acts of worship and community celebrations.

    c. seven in number.

    (d.) invisible signs.

4. Through the sacrament of Baptism we

    a. receive the Holy Spirit.

    (b.) are kept from sin forever.

    c. are reborn as children of God.

    d. become members of the Church.

5. Through the sacrament of Confirmation we

    a. are anointed with holy oil.

    b. receive the Spirit in a new way.

    (c.) have water poured on our head as a sign of cleansing.

    d. are strengthened with special gifts of the Spirit.

C. Answer as thoughtfully and fully as you can.

1. What signs do you see that God is truly present and active in our world today?

(Some ideas that should be mentioned: the goodness of

people; service given freely to others.)

_____

_____

2. As a member of the Church what do you think your response should be to acts of racism and hate?

These are sinful attitudes that must be overcome in

ourselves.

_____

_____

3. Explain in your own words how Jesus acts in and through the sacraments.

In the sacraments we meet Jesus Christ, who welcomes,

strengthens, feeds, heals, and sends us out to serve.

_____

_____

4. What does it mean to you to be a witness to Christ? In other words, what would a person see or hear or sense in you that would show that you are a Catholic?

(Accept all responses.)

_____

_____

_____

5. Reflect for a moment on a problem or decision you and other young people must face or make in today's world. How can your faith help you?

(Accept all answers.)

_____

_____

_____

_____

Semester 1 Test

A. Choose the correct term to complete the statements.

Sacraments   Inspiration

Revelation   Bible

Apostles   Messiah

Grace   Genesis

Church   Tradition

1. __Church__ is the community of believers who follow the teachings of Jesus Christ.

2. __Apostles__ were those chosen by Jesus to help begin the Church.

3. __Messiah__ means "God's anointed one," the Savior.

4. __Genesis__ is the first book of the Bible.

5. __Revelation__ is God telling us about God's own Self.

6. __Inspiration__ is the special guidance of God under which the Bible was written.

7. __Bible__ is the book that contains God's word for us.

8. __Tradition__ refers to the truths and beliefs that have come to us from the time of Jesus and the apostles.

9. __Grace__ is God's life and love in our lives that can only be lost by serious sin.

10. __Sacraments__ are effective signs of Jesus' presence in the church.

B. Describe in your own words these mysteries and beliefs of our Catholic Church.

1. The Incarnation: __The Son of God took on our human__ nature and dwelt with us.

2. The Blessed Trinity: __The mystery of three Persons__ in one God: Father, Son, and Holy Spirit.

3. The Annunciation: __The event told in Luke's Gospel__ of the angel's visit to Mary announcing that she would be the Mother of God.

4. Pentecost: __The day on which the Holy Spirit came upon__ the apostles, fifty days after Easter.

5. Easter: __The day on which Jesus Christ rose from the__ dead.

C. Circle the letter beside the *correct* response.

1. We become members of the Church through the sacrament of

    a. Holy Orders.

    b. Grace.

    (c.) Baptism.

    d. Eucharist.

2. The part of the Bible in which we read about God and the early Israelites is the

   (a.) Old Testament.

   b. New Testament.

   c. Gospels.

   d. Revelation.

3. Faith is

   a. just another way of looking at life.

   (b.) a belief in things unseen.

   c. one of the sacraments.

   d. a feast of the Church.

4. The first sin of the human race is called

   (a.) original sin.

   b. mortal sin.

   c. venial sin.

   d. social sin.

5. The Council of Chalcedon proclaimed as a truth of faith that Jesus Christ

   a. was a great man.

   b. was obedient to His parents.

   c. lived among us.

   (d.) is both human and divine.

D. Answer as completely and thoughtfully as you can.

1. What do we learn from the New Testament that tells us Jesus Christ was truly human? truly God's Son?

   truly human _He was born of Mary; was obedient to His_

   parents; experienced hunger, thirst, sadness, happiness,

   death.

   Son of God _He forgave sins; worked miracles, restored_

   life to the dead.

2. Tell some of the images Jesus used to describe the Kingdom of God.

   A tiny seed that grows into a great tree; yeast that makes

   bread rise; a buried treasure; a pearl; a net that

   catches many fish.

3. The story of Adam and Eve shows us the elements of sin. Explain.

   Temptation suggests certain choices will make us happy; we

   give in to temptation; we must accept the consequences of

   our choice.

4. What does the story of Jesus' resurrection mean to you? What hope does it give you?

   Suffering and death will have no power over us. We too will

   rise again.

5. How did the Holy Spirit help the first followers of Jesus? How is the Holy Spirit helping you?

   The Holy Spirit strengthened and encouraged the disciples

   to follow Jesus. (Accept appropriate responses)

10 THE EUCHARIST

Birthdays, graduations, holidays—why do human beings seem to have a need to celebrate and remember?

Why do we need to say: we were here; we did this; this event or person was important to us?

What are the most important celebrations in your life? What do they help you to remember and celebrate?

People often celebrate around a table and at a meal. There we call to mind a happy memory, an important person, or some event that has deep meaning for us. Think of a typical Thanksgiving Day celebration in our country. Is Thanksgiving celebrated in the same way as the Fourth of July? Why or why not?

_____

_____

_____

_____

_____

How do people of faith remember and celebrate all that God has done for us?

What do you think is the best way for Catholics to remember all that Jesus did?

_____

_____

_____

_____

_____

NOTE: The Eucharist should be the center of Catholic life. Help the young people come to a greater appreciation for and participation in it. Use this chapter and the next to reinforce these ideas.

1 Jesus gave Himself to us in the Eucharist at the Last Supper.

STRESS the underlined copy.

In the Bible we read of many celebrations among the Israelites. Sacrifice was one of their chief forms of celebrating and worshiping the one true God. At their celebrations, they remembered their past great moments of victory and deliverance, but there was one sacrifice and one celebration more important to them than all others. In this celebration and sacrifice, they remembered how God had freed them from slavery in Egypt by helping them to escape from the Egyptians.

On the night before this escape, the Israelites would be saved from the death of their newborns if they did as their leader Moses told them. Speaking in God's name, Moses ordered each Israelite family to kill a young lamb and then to sprinkle its blood on the doorposts and lintels of their homes. The angel of death, Moses told them, would see the blood and *pass over* their homes. Their newborn children would not die. Through Moses, God told the people to remember and to celebrate this saving event always.

There were strict rules about how this event was to be celebrated. The Israelites were to gather at a special meal consisting of unleavened bread, wine, bitter herbs, and a young lamb. The people were told:

> Each of you is to choose a lamb or a young goat and kill it, so that your families can celebrate Passover. Take a sprig of hyssop, dip it in the bowl containing the animal's blood, and wipe the blood on the doorposts and the beam over the door of your house. . . .When your children ask you, "What does this ritual mean?" you will answer, "It is the sacrifice of Passover to honor the Lord, because the Lord passed over the houses of the Israelites in Egypt."
> From Exodus 12:21–22, 26–27

During this **Passover** meal the Israelites thanked God for saving them. At last they were freed by God's power from their slavery in Egypt. Their Passover meals from then on would celebrate their deliverance from slavery to freedom.

Centuries later, Jesus participated in this same Passover meal with His disciples. He did this at the Last Supper on the night before He died. At the meal Jesus explained that His life would be sacrificed. Through the shedding of His blood, the community of believers would be saved from sin and death. Through Jesus, there would be a new and everlasting covenant with God.

The Last Supper of Jesus and His disciples was something very different from all the other Passover meals that had been celebrated. Here is the way Luke's Gospel describes part of it:

> Then he took a piece of bread, gave thanks to God, broke it, and gave it to them, saying, "This is my body, which is given for you. Do this in memory of me." In the same way, he gave them the cup after the supper, saying, "This cup is God's new covenant sealed with my blood, which is poured out for you."
> Luke 22:19–20

The bread and wine were now the **Eucharist**, or gift of thanks to God. The bread and wine still looked and tasted like bread and wine, but they were now what Jesus said they were: His very Body, His very Blood.

Christ told His disciples to repeat in His memory what He had done at the Last Supper. They would do this in the Eucharist, the sacrament of Christ's Body and Blood.

At every celebration of the Eucharist, we gather to give thanks to God. Through this sacred meal, we remember what Jesus did for us in His death and resurrection.

DISCUSS: The differences between the Passover and the Last Supper.

2 We celebrate the Eucharist at Mass.

ASK: What does the word "eucharist" mean?

Very shortly after the resurrection the small community of believers began to do what Jesus told them in remembrance of Him. Their celebrations consisted of listening to the Scriptures, reflecting on them, and recognizing Jesus' presence in the Eucharist. They worshiped together as one people united in the risen Christ. They were one people, sharing the one bread and the one cup and forming the one body of Christ.

Today we continue this celebration of the Eucharist at the **Mass**. The Mass is the Church's great prayer of praise and thanks to God. That is why the Church requires that all its members join together to take part in the Mass every Saturday evening or Sunday. *Mass* is a word that means to be "sent out." We are sent out from the table of the Lord to live as the followers of Christ.

When we take part in our parish's weekly celebration of the Eucharist:

- we join together to share in the great deeds of Jesus Christ by which He saved us;
- we each take part in the events we call to mind and draw strength from them;
- we renew our covenant with God and are nourished in this great sacrament;
- and we resolve to live as God's loving children.

Our celebration of Mass on the Lord's Day (Sunday) is the most important action of our week as Catholics and faithful followers of Jesus Christ.

Why do the followers of Christ celebrate the Eucharist? (in remembrance of Christ)

Why should we take part in the Mass at least every Sunday (or Saturday evening)?

(Because the Mass is the Church's great prayer of praise and thanks to God.)

ASK: Why is the eucharistic assembly so important? Why is the Eucharist not celebrated by just one person?

The Last Supper by Salvador Dali

3 The Eucharist is both a sacrifice and a meal.

The Eucharist gives our lives purpose, meaning, and hope if we are open to Jesus Christ, who comes to us under the forms of bread and wine.

As Catholics we know that the Eucharist, our great prayer of thanksgiving, is both a meal and a sacrifice.

- It is a meal because Jesus gave us the Eucharist at the Passover supper. Jesus said to His disciples, "Take and eat." "Take and drink."

- It is a sacrifice because it is a memorial of the passion, death, and resurrection of the Lord. It is the sacrifice of Jesus giving Himself totally for us on the cross. The bread broken and eaten, the cup "poured out" in death for us are ritual signs of Jesus' sacrificial offering to the Father.

And what should our response be when we share in the celebration of the Eucharist, a sacrament of love?

Discuss the reason for the eucharistic fast.

Listen to the Church's teaching that comes to us from the Second Vatican Council:

> The Church . . . earnestly desires that Christ's faithful when present at this mystery of faith, should not be there as strangers or silent spectators. On the contrary, through a proper appreciation of the rites and prayers, they should participate knowingly, devoutly, and actively. They should be instructed by God's word and be refreshed at the table of the Lord's body; they should give thanks to God; by offering the Immaculate Victim, not only through the hands of the priest, but also with him, they should learn to offer themselves too.

Constitution on the Sacred Liturgy, 48

What do we mean when we say that the Mass is both a meal and a sacrifice? (See bulleted items.)

What can you do to participate in the Mass more "knowingly, devoutly, actively?"

(Accept appropriate responses.)

STRESS again the nature of the eucharistic assembly.

Do You Know

As a sign of respect and reverence for the Eucharist, the Church asks us not to take any food or drink (except water) for one hour before receiving Holy Communion. This is known as the eucharistic fast.

Church Teachings About the Eucharist

- The Eucharist is one of the three Sacraments of Initiation.

- Jesus Christ is present in the Eucharist under the appearance of bread and wine.

- The Eucharist is a memorial of Jesus' saving death and resurrection.

- The mystery by which the bread and wine become the Body and Blood of Christ is called **transubstantiation**.

- The eucharistic celebration is called the Mass, which is both a meal and a sacrifice.

Prayer

Leader: The Lord Jesus, on the night He was betrayed, took a piece of bread, gave thanks to God, broke it, and said, "This is My Body, which is for you. Do this in memory of Me."

All: We remember, Lord Jesus, and we thank You.

Leader: In the same way, after the supper He took the cup and said, "This cup is God's new covenant, sealed in My Blood. Whenever you drink it, do so in memory of Me."

All: We remember, Lord Jesus, and we thank You.

Leader: This means that every time we eat this Bread and drink from this cup we proclaim the Lord's death until He comes.

All: Come, Lord Jesus.

Reflection and Action

Words to Remember

Find and define the following.

Eucharist The Body and Blood of Christ under the appearances of bread and wine.

Passover The meal celebrated by the Jews in memory of their deliverance from slavery in Egypt.

Things to Think About

Why do you think Catholics feel that the Eucharist is so important?

What do the words of Jesus "Do this in memory of Me" tell us about how important the Eucharist was in Jesus' eyes?

How was Jesus responding to our deep human need to celebrate what is most important to us?

Things to Share

Imagine that you are at the Last Supper. You watch and listen as Jesus takes the bread and then the wine and says over them His unforgettable words. With all that you know now, what would you like to tell Him? What do you think He might say to you? Share some of your thoughts in your journal.

11 THE MASS

Somehow the giving of gifts is very important to human beings.
When and why do you give gifts? What makes a gift a GIFT?

In some parts of the world there are so few priests that the Mass is celebrated only once a year. Catholics at these mission churches eagerly await that one day as if it were their favorite holiday. Many arrive hours before the Mass begins. They want to be prepared for the Great Event.

Most of us live in places where Mass is celebrated at least every weekend. Sometimes we forget to prepare for it. Other times we arrive at the last minute—and even wish we were someplace else! Unless we remind ourselves of its meaning and importance, the Mass can become for us the Gift Unseen.

Is the Mass often a gift unseen in your life?
(Do not ask for public response.)
Have there been times when you recognized the Mass as a gift? Tell about those times.
(Encourage the young people to respond.)

_____

_____

_____

_____

_____

_____

NOTE: If some young people have experienced different rites or styles of liturgy, invite them to share their own stories.

1 In the Liturgy of the Word we listen to God's word from the Bible.

The Mass, our celebration of the Eucharist, should be the Great Event each week for Catholics. It is the central act of worship, or **liturgy**, in the Catholic Church.

In every corner of the world, Catholics gather for the celebration of the Mass, to raise their voices as a faith community in praise and thanksgiving to God. We can hear the words of Mass spoken in every language. But the basic structure of the Mass is always the same, no matter where we are on earth.

The Mass has two principal parts: the Liturgy of the Word and the Liturgy of the Eucharist. However, before the Liturgy of the Word, the Mass begins with the Introductory Rites. These include the entrance procession; the greeting by the priest; the penitential rite, during which we ask for God's mercy; and the Glory to God prayer. After the opening prayer by the priest, we are ready to begin the Liturgy of the Word.

During the Liturgy of the Word we hear God's word proclaimed to us from the Bible. In each of three readings, we listen as a parish family and open our hearts as God speaks to us and guides us.

The Bible readings for each Mass are chosen by the Church to help us celebrate each Sunday and season. The book that has all the readings we use at Mass is called the *Lectionary.* It is not the Bible, but it uses parts of the Bible. During the Liturgy of the Word:

- The first reading at Mass is most often from the Old Testament.

- The second reading is from the New Testament (but not from the Gospels).

- The third reading is always from one of the four Gospels (Matthew, Mark, Luke, John).

After the readings, the priest or deacon gives a homily, or explanation, to help us understand better God's word and how to live it. Then we stand together and profess our faith in the words of the Creed.

The Liturgy of the Word then concludes with the General Intercessions, or Prayers of the Faithful. Here we remember the needs of the Church, the world, those who suffer and who are in need, and our local community.

Having been nourished at the table of God's word, we are now ready to celebrate the Liturgy of the Eucharist.

What is the Liturgy of the Word? How can we take part more fully in each week's Liturgy of the Word? (By preparing in advance; by listening carefully.)

2 In the Liturgy of the Eucharist we offer and receive the gift of Jesus.

The second principal part of the Mass is the Liturgy of the Eucharist, and it begins with the presentation and preparation of the gifts of bread and wine. These are simple, basic elements of human life that Jesus used at the Last Supper.

Our gifts of bread and wine are presented to the priest. The priest accepts these gifts and prepares them at the altar. They will become for us the Body and Blood of Christ. We also bring our own lives—our brokenness and needs, as well as our joys. We join them to those of Jesus.

During this preparation, we also may offer money or other gifts for the Church and the poor. These are put in a special place, but not on the altar.

The priest then begins what is called the *Eucharistic Prayer.* It is the heart of the celebration of the Mass. In this prayer we lift up our hearts in praise and thanksgiving to God through Jesus Christ. As the word *Eucharist* reminds us, we give *thanks* to God the Father for all our blessings, especially for the Son of God.

The priest prays that through the power of the Holy Spirit the bread and wine will be changed and become the Body and Blood of Christ. Now the priest does and says what Jesus did at the Last Supper and what He asked us to do in memory of Him. The priest says over the bread, "This is my body," and over the wine, "This is my blood." This is called the *consecration.*

The Church gathered together at each Mass offers this sacrifice of Christ to God the Father in the Holy Spirit. After praying for our needs and the members of the Church, both living and dead, we raise our voices in joyful praise and sing "Amen." The great Eucharistic Prayer is now finished.

Before we come forward to receive Communion, we pray the Lord's Prayer and offer one another a sign of the peace of Christ that we are called to share. Then, following what Jesus Himself did, the priest breaks the Eucharistic Bread that we will share. As he does this we pray the Lamb of God prayer. Those who are prepared reverently receive Communion, either in the hand or on the tongue. Our response just before receiving communion is "Amen."

In this **Holy Communion** we are nourished with the sacrament of the Eucharist. We are made one with Christ and one another. We are no longer many: we are now one in the love of Christ.

What gift do we offer to God at our eucharistic assembly?   (bread, wine, our own lives)

What gift does God offer us in return?
(the Body and Blood of Christ)

DEFINE and DISCUSS: Eucharist, consecration, Holy Communion, Mass.

Do You Know

Through history the celebration of the Eucharist has been called by many different names. Some of them are "the breaking of the bread," "the Lord's Supper," and the name "Eucharist" itself, which means thanksgiving. The name most often used is "Mass," a word taken from the Latin word for "sending forth." The emphasis is on the gathered assembly now being sent forth to bring Jesus Christ to others by loving and serving the Lord in everyone, especially "the least" of His brothers and sisters.

3 At the end of Mass we are sent forth to bring God's love to others.

At the end of Mass, the priest blesses the assembly and says, "Go in peace to love and serve the Lord." This is the peace that Jesus promised His friends. This is the peace that the world cannot give: the peace of Christ.

The Church sends us away from the celebration of the Mass in the peace of Christ. But our work is not finished. We are to live the Mass by loving and serving the Lord in other people.

Some of the ways we might love Christ in others are: SHARE ideas on how we can accomplish these challenges.

- share our time and talents with them;

- help others experience God's love in and through us, as shown by our faith and generosity;

- avoid all forms of injustice and prejudice based on race, sex, or nationality;

- respect our bodies and the bodies of others as temples of the Holy Spirit;

- strive daily to grow closer to God and to all of God's people.

We should also remember that we are followers of Jesus Christ, who came not to be served, but to serve. Some of the ways we might serve the Lord are:

- care for the poor, the sick, and the lonely;

- respect life, especially the dignity of human life;

- make the joy and peace of Christ visible in our lives for all to see.

At Mass our gifts of bread and wine are changed into the Body and Blood of Christ. Through the Mass, the celebration of this sacrament, we hope and pray that we, too, may be changed into faithful signs of Christ.

The next time you go to Mass, how will you take part?   (Encourage appropriate responses.)

How will you live the Mass in your family? among your friends?   (See listed items.)

STRESS: After celebrating Mass, we are sent out to be signs of Christ's love to others.

ASSIGN for review and home study.

Church Teachings About the Mass

- At the Mass, the celebration of the Eucharist, we gather for the central act of worship in the Catholic Church.

- The Mass has two principal parts: the Liturgy of the Word and the Liturgy of the Eucharist.

- The Liturgy of the Word consists of Scripture readings from the Old and New Testaments. The third reading is always taken from the Gospel.

- During the Liturgy of the Eucharist, we give praise and thanks to God. Our gifts of bread and wine become the Body and Blood of Christ.

- At Mass we call to mind and celebrate the life, death, and resurrection of Jesus Christ, as He asked His disciples to do.

- The Mass is both a meal and a sacrifice.

Prayer

During the Mass we pray together using the words Jesus gave to His friends. Praying this prayer together is one more sign that we are one with Him and with one another.

> Our Father, who art in heaven,
> hallowed be Thy name;
> Thy kingdom come;
> Thy will be done on earth
> as it is in heaven.
> Give us this day our daily bread;
> and forgive us our trespasses
> as we forgive those
> who trespass against us;
> and lead us not into temptation
> but deliver us from evil. Amen.

Reflection and Action

Words to Remember

Find and define the following.

Mass The celebration of the Eucharist. _____

_____

_____

Liturgy The public worship of the Church. _____

_____

_____

Things to Think About

The Church calls on us to be active, not passive, in our participation in the Mass. To do this we may have to change our prayer habits.

Four words might sum up the four actions of an active participant in the eucharistic celebration. How might we perform these actions better?

- listen
- offer   Invite the young people to share their ideas.
- receive
- serve

Things to Share

All people everywhere are called upon to worship God. How fortunate we are to have the Mass and to celebrate the perfect sacrifice of love! Talk over with Jesus your feelings of gratitude for the chance to share in His offering in the Mass. In your jounal, write about how you will try to live the meaning of the Mass this week.

12 THE SACRAMENT OF RECONCILIATION

How do you react when other people hurt you or are unkind to you?

Do you forgive others? Do you accept the forgiveness of others?

Each of us has dreams and plans. To make our dreams and plans come true, we have to make choices in our lives. Pretend you have chosen one of the following careers. What would you do in each situation?

If you were a *lawyer,* what plans would you make to foster justice in the legal system? How would you help poor people get good lawyers?

If you were a *dancer,* what kind of dance company would you join? Where would you like to perform?

If you were an *Olympic athlete,* what world record would you try to break?

If you were a *carpenter,* what would you like to make?

If you were an *astronaut,* what kind of space travel would you like to use? What planet would you like to explore?

In all of the situations named above, people have to make choices. Would their decisions seriously affect the lives of others? How would they know that they made correct decisions? (1)

Some decisions are so important that they can affect every other part of our lives. Think of your life of faith. What decisions do you make that either help or hurt your life as a follower of Christ? (2)

(1) Allow time for thoughtful responses—drawing conclusions about decisions made.

(2) Do not insist on personal responses. This would make an excellent journal entry.

STRESS in this chapter the positive nature of the sacrament of Reconciliation and the role of the Church's ministry.

1 Sin separates us from God.

STRESS the underlined copy.

In the Gospels Jesus told us a story about a young man who made some very definite decisions. The young man was looking forward to a life of fun, adventure, and independence. He forgot, however, that choices always have consequences. Our decisions affect not only ourselves but those around us. Here is the young man's story.

There was once a man who had two sons. The younger one said to him, "Father, give me my share of the property now." So the man divided his property between his two sons. After a few days the younger son sold his part of the property and left home with the money. He went to a country far away, where he wasted his money in reckless living. He spent everything he had.
Luke 15:11–14

In sinning we willingly make choices that do harm to ourselves and others. Our love relationship with God is weakened by our unwillingness to live as God calls us to live. When we sin, we turn away from God and turn toward something that is not God. **Sin** is freely choosing to do something we know is wrong and against God's will.

DISCUSS the last sentence as a definition of sin.

Even though the young man in the story chose a life of sin, he apparently had not taken time to examine his life. At first, he did not seem to see the harm he was doing to himself. But the young man was eventually forced to come face to face with it, as you will see in the next part of his story.

Then a severe famine spread over that country, and he was left without a thing. So he went to work for one of the citizens of that country, who sent him out to his farm to take care of the pigs. He wished he could fill himself with the bean pods the pigs ate, but no one gave him anything to eat. At last he came to his senses and said, "All my father's hired workers have more than they can eat, and here I am about to starve! I will get up and go to my father and say, 'Father, I have sinned against God and against you. I am no longer fit to be called your son; treat me as one of your hired workers.'" So he got up and started back to his father.
Luke 15:14–20

ACT OUT the gospel story with volunteers.

Do You Know

In order for a sin to be a mortal sin, three conditions are necessary:

- the sinful action or attitude must do serious harm to our relationship with God, others, or ourself;

- we must have clear knowledge and know full well that what we choose will do serious harm;

- we must freely choose and intend to do this serious evil.

All three conditions must be met for any sin to be considered mortal.

As he made his way home, the young man surely must have wondered how his father was going to treat him when he confessed that he led a sinful and reckless life and was now penniless. But any feeling of doubt vanished when the following happened:

He was still a long way from home when his father saw him; his heart was filled with pity, and he ran, threw his arms around his son, and kissed him. "Father," the son said, "I have sinned against God and against you. I am no longer fit to be called your son." But the father called to his servants. "Hurry!" he said. "Bring the best robe and put it on him. Put a ring on his finger and shoes on his feet. Then go and get the prize calf and kill it, and let us celebrate with a feast! For this son of mine was dead, but now he is alive; he was lost, but now he has been found." And so the feasting began.
Luke 15:20–24

Although the young man had made a poor choice, the father still welcomed him with great joy and love. He could not wait to have his son restored, or brought back, to him—to be *reconciled* with him.

The father loved the son so much. It was not just a romantic kind of love. We call the kind of love he had for his son unconditional love—the father did not want, or ask for, an explanation. He reached out in love to accept his son.

Jesus told the story to let us know how God loves and forgives us. As we shall see, we experience God's mercy in a special way through the wonderful sacrament of Reconciliation.

What do you think about the father's reaction in Jesus' story?

DEFINE the word *reconciliation*.

DISCUSS how this sacrament helps us on our ongoing journey of faith.

2 We examine our conscience before Reconciliation.

At times we realize that we are going in the wrong direction. But we do not have to wait until we have had an experience as bad as the young man had. We can check our direction often by examining our conscience. **Conscience** is the ability we have to decide whether an action is right or wrong. We ask the Holy Spirit to help us judge the direction in which our life is now going. Rooted in the faith of the Church, we are called upon to continue forming our conscience throughout life. Seeking advice from holy and wise people is one way of doing this.

When we examine our conscience, we honestly ask ourselves about our relationship with God and others. For example:

- Am I strengthening my relationship with God through prayer and the sacraments?
- Am I trying to grow as a follower of Christ and member of the Church?
- Have I done harm to myself by using alcohol or drugs?
- Have I treated others fairly and honestly?

Sin is always a personal choice. At times, sin can also be described as a choice of society. This is what we mean by social sin, such as prejudice based on race, age, or gender.

When we examine our conscience, we understand that there are different types of sin. When we deliberately choose to completely break off our whole relationship with God, we call this **mortal sin**. Mortal sin is very serious. Less serious sin is called **venial sin**.

Our world is a challenging place in which to live and we can often be tempted to do what is wrong. But a **temptation** is not a sin. It is an attraction to sin. Everyone is tempted. That is why we need God's grace to be strong in making good choices.

DISCUSS the difference between a temptation and a sin.

Sin always affects more than just one person. It also affects the community—it can even affect the world. Through Jesus' death and resurrection, the power of sin has been overcome. Now we try to heal the hurt caused by sin. We express our true sorrow and receive God's mercy through the ministry of the Church. We celebrate this great message of hope in the sacrament of Reconciliation.

What is the difference between temptation and sin?

3 Reconciliation is a sacrament of God's mercy.

DEFINE the sacrament of Reconciliation.

We all have a loving Father in God. To show unconditional love, God has given us the **sacrament** of **Reconciliation.** In this sacrament, through the grace and mercy of God, we re-establish the friendship between us and God and the entire Christian community. We celebrate God's love and forgiveness and our love and forgiveness of one another.

Before we celebrate the sacrament of Reconciliation, we take time to examine our conscience. We do not have to remember every little fault. We should focus on a main weakness or serious sins that separate us from God's life of grace. We may want to discuss this with the priest.

We can celebrate the sacrament of Reconciliation in one of two ways: individually with the priest in the *Individual Rite;* or with members of the community and a priest in the *Communal Rite.*

Individual Rite

The priest greets me.

I make the sign of the cross.
The priest asks me to trust in God's mercy.

He or I may read something from the Bible.

I talk with the priest about myself. I confess my sins: what I did wrong and why.

The priest talks to me about loving God and others.

He gives me a penance.

I make an Act of Contrition. In the name of God and the Church, the priest gives me absolution. (He may extend or place his hands on my head.) This means that my sins have been forgiven.

Together, the priest and I give thanks for God's forgiveness and love.

Communal Rite

We sing an opening hymn and the priest greets us.

The priest prays an opening prayer.

We listen to a reading from the Bible and a homily.

We examine our conscience.

We make an Act of Contrition.

We may pray a litany or sing a song. We then pray the Our Father.

We confess our sins to a priest. In the name of God and the Christian community, the priest gives us a penance and absolution.

We pray as we conclude our celebration. The priest blesses us, and we go in the peace and joy of Christ.

This sacrament is a wonderful way to praise and thank God for the gifts of mercy and forgiveness. It is also a way to grow in God's life of grace and in the love of one another.

Have you ever been reconciled with another person? How?

Why do we call the sign of God's love and forgiveness the sacrament of Reconciliation?

Church Teachings: Reconciliation

- Christ has entrusted to His Church the power to forgive sins. "Receive the Holy Spirit," Jesus told His disciples. "If you forgive people's sins, they are forgiven: if you do not forgive them, they are not forgiven" (John 20:22–3).

- In the sacrament of Reconciliation, our sins are forgiven; we are reconciled to God, the Church, and one another.

- What is confessed is protected by the seal of confession, which obliges the priest to total secrecy.

Prayer

Lord Jesus, have mercy on me a sinner.

STRESS the importance of preparing for the sacrament of Reconciliation. Encourage young people to take advantage of the sacrament throughout their lives. Help them to be familiar especially with the Individual Rite.

Reflection and Action

Words to Remember

Find and define the following.

conscience The ability to judge between right and wrong.

_____

_____

sin Freely choosing to do what we know is wrong and against God's will.

_____

_____

sacrament of Reconciliation The sacrament through which by the grace and mercy of God we re-establish the friendship between us and God and the Christian community.

Things to Think About

Are you ever inclined to avoid being reconciled with God, the Church, or someone else? What excuses do you feel tempted to use to "put things off"?

What can you do to make yourself a reconciler instead of an obstacle to reconciliation? Write some of your reflections in your journal.

Things to Share

In the sacrament of Reconciliation, we celebrate God's mercy. It is also a wonderful opportunity to unburden ourselves. We can experience healing and grow from this meeting with the merciful Christ, who knows our weaknesses and still loves and forgives us.

Talk over with Jesus your feelings in experiencing this forgiving love.

Unit 3 Test

A. Write each term next to the definition that defines it.

Eucharist   Holy Communion

Passover   Consecration

Mass   Lectionary

Conscience   Liturgy of the Word

Reconciliation   Liturgy of the Eucharist

1. __Reconciliation__ is the sacrament in which we experience God's mercy and forgiveness.

2. __Mass__ is the celebration of the Eucharist. The word means "sent out."

3. __Passover__ is the celebration of the freedom of the Israelites from slavery in Egypt.

4. __Holy Communion__ takes place when we receive and are nourished by the Eucharist.

5. __Lectionary__ is the collection of readings that are proclamed at Mass.

6. __Liturgy of the Word__ is the part of the Mass during which we hear God's word proclaimed.

7. __Conscience__ is the ability we have to judge whether an action is right or wrong.

8. __Liturgy of the Eucharist__ is the part of the Mass in which we offer and receive the gift of Jesus.

9. __Eucharist__ is the sacrament of the Body and Blood of Christ.

10. __Consecration__ is the part of the Mass when the priest says and does what Jesus did at the Last Supper.

B. Circle the response that does *not* belong.

1. On the first Passover the Israelites

   a. refused to listen to Moses, their leader.

   b. killed a young lamb.

   c. sprinkled the lamb's blood on their doorposts.

   d. waited for the angel of death to pass over.

2. On the night before He died, Jesus

   a. celebrated Passover with His friends.

   b. explained to them that His life would be sacrificed.

   c. died on the cross.

   d. gave us the Eucharist.

3. When we celebrate Mass we

   a. share in Jesus' life, death, and resurrection.

   b. renew our covenant with God.

   c. promise to live as God's loving children.

   d. are freed from original sin.

4. In the sacrament of Reconciliation

   a. our sins are forgiven.

   b. we are reconciled to God.

   c. we experience God's mercy.

   d. we are obligated to secrecy.

5. The Eucharist is

   a. our initiation into the church.

   b. a meal because Jesus said, "Take and eat it."

   c. a sacrifice because it is a memorial of Jesus' death.

   d. The church's great prayer of thanksgiving.

C. Answer as thoughtfully and as fully as you can.

1. How did Jesus want His disciples to remember Him?

By repeating in His memory what He did at the Last Supper.

2. What would help you understand and participate more fully in the Mass?

(Accept appropriate responses.)

3. At the end of Mass we are "sent forth" to love and serve others. What does that mean to you?

Mass is not intended to be a private prayer. The Eucharist

calls us to care for others, as Christ cares for us.

4. What can you do to help yourself "form your conscience," which means to make better choices between right and wrong?

Possible response: take time to examine my conscience to

become more aware of the choices I make.

5. What is the difference between a temptation and a sin?

A temptation is an attraction to sin. A sin is a deliberate

choice to do what one knows is wrong.

13 LIVING GOD'S LAW

Why do we need laws anyway? Do you need laws in your life?

If you could make one law for the whole world, what would it be?

PEXPERIENCE: Are laws necessary? Why? Do laws keep us from being free? Or do they guarantee freedom?

Parents usually make rules because they are concerned about their children. Some children insist upon hearing over and over why certain rules have to be followed. Always having to give reasons and always having to accept them may not be easy for parents or young people.

Think about your own life. How well do you accept rules and the reasons for those rules?

Write down some of the rules that you are asked to follow in your home. Give a reason why you think each rule was made.

The Rules

(The group should have no difficulty coming up with these.)

_____

_____

_____

_____

_____

The Reasons

(Young people might have more difficulty understanding the

reasons for rules. They are at an age where they feel they

should be making their own rules.)

_____

_____

_____

Do rules or laws restrict freedom or foster it?

In your opinion, no matter who makes rules or laws, how do you at this time in your life judge a good one from a bad one? (1)

Does any law that comes from God have special value in your life? Which one? (2)

(1) This is an important question. Help the group develop a criterion for judging rules.

(2) Help the young people to distinguish between what is a law and what is not.

85

The Ten Commandments

1. I am the Lord your God, who brought you out of slavery. Worship no god except Me.

2. You shall not misuse the name of the Lord your God.

3. Remember to keep holy the Sabbath day.

4. Honor your father and your mother.

5. You shall not kill.

6. You shall not commit adultery.

7. You shall not steal.

8. You shall not tell lies against your neighbor.

9. You shall not want to take your neighbor's wife or husband.

10. You shall not want to take your neighbor's possessions.

From Exodus 20:1–17

DISCUSS: Why did God give the Ten Commandments to the Israelites?
Why do we say the first three commandments deal with our relationship to God?

1 The Ten Commandments teach us how to live as God's people.

STRESS the underlined copy.

Over and over again, God reached out with love to the Israelites. From the Old Testament we learn that God wanted to form them into a holy people, a nation that would be set apart. And God would do this by entering into a covenant with them. A **covenant** is a special agreement between God and people.

The Israelites cherished one very important covenant. This was the covenant God made on Mount Sinai with their great leader **Moses**, who lead the Israelites out of slavery in Egypt. The reason for this covenant was that God wanted them to be free, not only from physical and political bondage, but from the spiritual slavery of sin as well.

God explained to Moses the responsibilities that the Israelites would have in observing the covenant. And the Israelites agreed to accept them. These responsibilities were summarized in what we now call the Ten Commandments. The **Ten Commandments** are laws about how to respect, honor, and love God and others.

The Catholic Church teaches that the Ten Commandments are God's law for us, too, and they may not be changed by any human law. We believe that by observing the Ten Commandments we grow in freedom. We see that the first three commandments deal more specifically with our direct relationship to God. The remaining seven deal with our relationship to one another.

The **First Commandment** reminds us that we worship and serve the one true God. We put God first in our lives and reject false gods, such as the exaggerated desire for power, wealth, or popularity. When we live by the spirit of this commandment, we do not put our trust in superstitious or occult practices. We place our faith in God.

The **Second Commandment** is directed to the honor of God's name, and also helps us to appreciate the gifts of speech and communication, using them with care and respect. Christians should also show special reverence for the name of Jesus Christ.

As Catholics, we observe the **Third Commandment** by participating in the celebration of Mass on the Lord's Day— Sunday or Saturday evening—and by keeping that day holy, especially in prayer and by refraining from unnecessary work. In God's wisdom, we are reminded that we need rest.

NOTE: The young people should know the Ten Commandments by heart.

86

2 The Ten Commandments also teach us how to live with one another.

The **Fourth Commandment** teaches us to honor, obey, and care for our parents. We should also show respect and honor for older people and those in authority. Christians reflect on the way that Jesus showed love and respect toward Mary and Joseph.

The **Fifth Commandment** teaches us to respect the sacredness of life, especially human life. We are to avoid anything—murder, abortion, suicide, mercy killing—that would deny the dignity or respect given to God's gift of life. We believe that every human being from the beginning of life in its mother's womb has the God-given right to life. The Church teaches us that there is no excuse for human interference in God's authority over life.

In a world torn apart by violence, war, and ethnic strife, the Church has voiced its opposition to armed conflict as a solution to political and social problems. In recent years, the popes and the American bishops have spoken out strongly against the use of horrific global weapons, both nuclear and chemical. God's law calls us to work untiringly for peace on earth, beginning in our own lives and extending in ever-widening circles to the whole human family.

NOTE: The young people should be able to explain clearly in their own words the responsibilities called for by each commandment.

Not only is direct killing of oneself or others against God's law, but anything that could injure or endanger life, such as uncontrolled anger, use of narcotics, excessive eating and drinking, neglecting proper care of one's health, and failing to take proper care of the environment in which life flourishes.

The **Sixth Commandment** condemns not only adultery—unfaithfulness in marriage—but also upholds the sacredness of the gift of sexuality given to us by God. This gift must never be used in a way contrary to God's plan. Our bodies are temples of the Holy Spirit, and as such must be respected by ourselves and others. To treat the gift of human sexuality with selfishness or disrespect is to ignore the beauty and wonder that God gave to us as sharers in creation. Anything that cheapens or lessens this gift is against God's law.

The commandment also reminds us that we must never be afraid of our human sexuality, because it is something truly beautiful. If we are concerned or worried about something as we grow older, we should seek advice and counsel from our parents and other competent authorities.

The **Seventh Commandment** deals with justice in all its forms. It upholds the right of all people to share in God's gifts and to have respect as equals in the presence of the Creator. We are to have a special care for the poor and avoid amassing things for their own sake. Stealing, cheating, and dishonesty in any form are against this commandment.

Wasting or misusing the earth's resources are also ways of ignoring this commandment. We are also reminded that jealousy and prejudice should have no place in our lives.

It is necessary to have truth if we are to live in a society of openness and honesty. The **Eighth Commandment** teaches us to respect the good name of all people and to avoid anything that would injure another's reputation. Lying, which is holding the truth from those who have a right to know it, is against the Christian way of life.

Invasion of privacy, harmful gossip, and betraying a trust are also against this commandment. Finally we must remember that prejudice in any form and for any reason—racial, sexual, or any other—is a failure to live the truth.

The **Ninth Commandment** deals with the control of our minds with regard to sexual matters. This commandment gives us a positive direction to help us not be preoccupied with our sexuality, which is important but only one dimension of our humanity. We should also remember that pornography in its many forms lessens human dignity and destroys the sacredness of our sexuality.

The **Tenth Commandment** warns us against envy or any willful desire to possess the property that belongs to others. Envy has no place in our lives and cannot lead us to true happiness. Jesus knew this and told us to "store up treasure in heaven."

Explain the statement "The Ten Commandments mean much more than meets the eye."

3 We are called to fulfill the Law of Love.

With God's laws, the people knew the right way to live. How well some people followed them was another story. In establishing the covenant and in giving the Ten Commandments, God wanted the people to observe them out of love for God and one another. The great prayer of the Israelites told them how to observe God's commandments:

Israel, remember this! The Lord—and the Lord alone—is our God. Love the Lord your God with all your heart, with all your soul, and with all your strength.
Deuteronomy 6:4–5

Along with loving God, the people were also told, "Love your neighbor as you love yourself" (Leviticus 19:18). The Ten Commandments were ways to show how to love God and neighbor.

Jesus knew the laws of His people and how they were to be observed. He respected them so much that He said, "Do not think that I have come to do away with the Law of Moses and the teachings of the prophets. I have not come to do away with them, but to make their teachings come true" (Matthew 5:17).

INVITE the group to learn Deuteronomy 6:4-5 by heart.

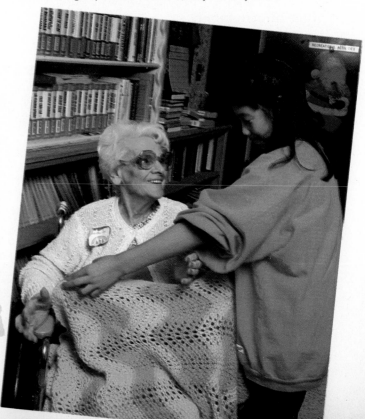

NOTE: If time allows, do a dramatic reading or roleplay of this story.

Do You Know

Once Jesus was asked, "Who is my neighbor?" As a wise teacher, Jesus told a story to help His followers understand, and that story is told in Luke 10:30–37. Read this beautiful story of the **Good Samaritan**, and see how well you understand Jesus' answer.

According to Luke's Gospel, one day a man came up to Jesus and said to Him, "Teacher, what must I do to receive eternal life?"

Jesus answered him, "What do the Scriptures say? How do you interpret them?"

The man replied, "'Love the Lord your God with all your heart, with all your soul, with all your strength, and with all your mind'; and 'love your neighbor as you love yourself.'"

Jesus said to the man, "You are right; do this and you will live."
From Luke 10:25–28

We call this wonderful teaching the **Law of Love**. How important Jesus thought it was to love God so totally and to love our neighbors as ourselves!

What do you think it means to love your neighbor as yourself?

Help the young people to reflect on the critical nature of self-esteem.

Church Teachings About God's Law

- The Ten Commandments guide us in our relationship with God and with one another. No human law can change them.

- The Ten Commandments are not mere rules; they are laws guiding us in living the covenant we have with God.

- Living according to the commandments is not optional. It is a serious responsibility — the only way to true happiness and peace.

Prayer

The laws of the Lord are right,
 and those who obey them are happy.
The commands of the Lord are just
 and give understanding to the mind.

Psalm 19:8

Words to Remember

Find and define the following.

covenant _A special agreement between God and people._

_____

_____

_____

Ten Commandments _Laws about how to respect,_ _honor, and love God and others._

_____

_____

_____

Law of Love (See page 88.) _____

_____

_____

_____

Things to Think About

It is sometimes fashionable to think of the Ten Commandments as a burden. This is to forget that their source and purpose is love. Which seems to you a better way to look at God's commandments: as restrictions on our freedom or as guidance in how to live and use our freedom? Why?

Things to Share

Knowing the purpose of God's law, has your idea of the Ten Commandments changed? How will you share a positive understanding of God's law with others? Use your journal to sketch your plans.

NOTE: Invite volunteers to share their reflections on God's law as experienced in the Ten Commandments and in the Law of Love.

14 JESUS' WAY OF LOVING

Why do people want to be happy?

Where do you find happiness in life?

In 1776 the writers of the Declaration of Independence spoke the most important values for a new country. Today Americans are proud to proclaim the values of life, liberty, and the pursuit of happiness.

When you stop to think about it, we probably know what we mean by life and liberty. But what do we mean by happiness? Write your thoughts here.

_____

_____

_____

_____

Whatever you may have answered, it is safe to say that happiness is basic. People do not trade happiness for something better, because there is nothing better!

One surprising thing about happiness is that true happiness seems to come to us as a kind of by-product. It comes to us when we are not selfish or self-centered. People have discovered that—oddly enough—we gain happiness when we give happiness away. What do you think this means?

_____

_____

_____

_____

What do you think our Catholic faith has to do with the pursuit of happiness? Do we have any guidelines in faith that will help us to find true happiness?

1 The Beatitudes are guidelines for true happiness.

STRESS the underlined copy.

In the time of Jesus, God's people were again in need of someone to lead them to true freedom. As a nation they had suffered through many wars and domination by foreign rulers. They were looking for the Messiah to free them from this oppression and to show them the path to true happiness.

God had given the Israelites the gift of the Law of Moses as their way of life, and Jesus wanted to teach again its lesson: love God and love neighbor. He told the people that His Father is the God of love, not of fear.

When Jesus spoke to the people, He sensed that their spirits were low. They had lost their way. Jesus challenged the people to take a giant step toward freedom, no matter how painful it seemed. Jesus promised that those who suffer for the sake of the Kingdom of God would be rewarded. At the very beginning of one of the best-known sections of Matthew's Gospel, called the **Sermon on the Mount**, we find Jesus' plan. We have come to call it the Beatitudes.

The **Beatitudes** are eight guidelines for true happiness given to us by Jesus. They promise freedom to live Jesus' way and teach us the spirit in which we are to live for God's Kingdom, or the *Kingdom of heaven* as it is called in Matthew's Gospel.

Jesus promised great rewards for those who would follow His ways of happiness. When we depend on God's love and not on possessions, when we show compassion, humility, and mercy, we are working to build up the Kingdom of God. This is also true when we work for justice and peace, even when this sometimes requires heroic effort on our part. How blessed and how happy shall we be!

Which of the Beatitudes challenges you most? Why?

The Beatitudes

Happy are those who know they are spiritually poor; the Kingdom of heaven belongs to them!

Happy are those who mourn; God will comfort them!

Happy are those who are humble; they will receive what God has promised!

Happy are those whose greatest desire is to do what God requires; God will satisfy them fully!

Happy are those who are merciful to others; God will be merciful to them!

Happy are the pure in heart; they will see God!

Happy are those who work for peace; they will be called God's children!

Happy are those who are persecuted because they do what God requires; the Kingdom of heaven belongs to them!

Matthew 5:3–10

ASK: How do the Beatitudes compare with your ideas about true happiness?

NOTE: Have some of the group, who have prepared in advance, do a dramatic reading of the Beatitudes.

92

2 Jesus gave us the new commandment to love one another as He has loved us.

When the disciples of Jesus looked back on His life and teaching, they were struck again and again with the importance Jesus put on love. By word and example, Jesus had urged them to love as He did.

He taught them first of all **to love God**. Everything that Jesus did was directed to God. We read that Jesus went off to the desert or to the mountains frequently to be alone with God and to pray. In fact, Jesus' whole life could be summed up as always doing the will of His Father.

Jesus taught His disciples **to love even their enemies**. He told them, "You have heard that it was said, 'Love your friends, hate your enemies.' But now I tell you: love your enemies and pray for those who persecute you, so that you may become the sons and daughters of your Father in heaven" (from Matthew 5:43–45).

This love of enemies is a real challenge. Think what kind of world we might have if the followers of Jesus Christ put this one teaching into practice.

Above all, Jesus taught His disciples **to love one another as He had loved them**. The night before Jesus died, He talked with His disciples during the Last Supper and gave them His "new commandment." This was His farewell to His friends, so His words take on a special urgency and importance.

> Now I give you a **new commandment**: love one another. As I have loved you, so you must love one another. If you have love for one another, then everyone will know that you are my disciples.
> John 13:34–35

Later on Jesus repeated His commandment and pointed to Himself as the perfect example of love for others. Jesus said to His disciples, "Love one another, just as I love you. The greatest love a person can have for friends is to give his or her life for them" (from John 15:12–13). What more could Jesus have done to show His love for God, for us, and for all His friends, even for His enemies?

What can you do to show others the love of Jesus Christ in your own life?

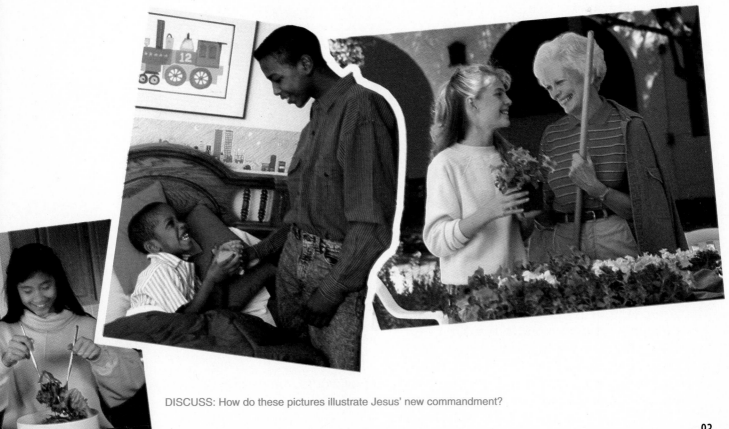

DISCUSS: How do these pictures illustrate Jesus' new commandment?

93

Do You Know

The virtues of faith, hope, and love are often called the **theological virtues** because they are gifts of God and help to direct our lives toward God.

3 Jesus calls us to follow Him in faith, hope, and love.

Christians of all times and places have tried to follow Jesus' new commandment, and Jesus Himself showed the way. He said, "I am the way, the truth, and the life" (John 14:6). But to be like Jesus, the early Christians discovered very quickly that this would mean a change in lifestyle. They would have to live a life of virtue.

A **virtue** is a habit of doing good, and three virtues stand out as the most important of all: faith, hope, and love. These are the virtues that mark a Christian way of life.

First of all, **faith** is a gift of God. Jesus Himself told us, "No one can come to me unless the Father who sent me draws that person to me" (from John 6:44). Through faith, we have a deep and abiding relationship with God, who loves us completely. In faith we accept all that God teaches us and reveals to us. We respond in faith by placing our trust in God and by seeking to do God's will in all things.

The virtue of **hope** is one that really keeps us going. It helps us to keep our trust in God, even when things are going badly. People of hope never give up on God, themselves, or on the relationship they have with God. They never give in to despair, the opposite of hope.

They know that, even when things look bad, evil will never overcome good, hatred will never extinguish love. This is the promise that Jesus made to us.

Like faith, hope is also a gift from God. The challenge of hope is not to sit and wait for things to happen. Hopeful people are always on the go, seeking ways to bring justice and peace to the waiting world. Hope helps us remember that our true destiny is to be happy forever with God.

All virtues grow as we practice them, and as Saint Paul reminds us, the greatest of these virtues is the gift of **love.** The love we are speaking about, however, is not romantic love, which can easily come and go. The love we are speaking of is the virtue of love. This virtue draws us into the closest and most intimate relationship we can have with God. This love we have for God can become a powerful force in our lives and in our world. It helps us to love even those who are known as our enemies.

To love others requires sacrifice, generosity, the ability to risk when reaching out to another, and often the ability to forgive others and to welcome forgiveness in our own lives.

The gift of love is all around us. Jesus has shown us how to recognize it and use it in the world, not just as an idea, but as our true way of life. This is the meaning of being called a Christian person, one who follows Jesus, the giver of the new commandment of love. Loving others does not mean that we always agree with them or that we compromise our Christian principles.

How would you describe the virtue of true love?

ASK: Do you think that the gift of love is all around us? Explain.

Church Teachings: Christian Living

- The Beatitudes are eight guidelines for true happiness given to us by Jesus.

- The Beatitudes are found in Matthew's Gospel at the beginning of the section called the Sermon on the Mount. The entire sermon can be found in Matthew 5—7.

- Jesus taught us to love our enemies and to love others as He loves us.

- A virtue is a habit of doing good. The three theological virtues are faith, hope, and love.

Prayer

Lord, make me an instrument of Your peace. Where there is hatred, let me sow love; where there is injury, pardon; where there is doubt, faith; where there is despair, hope; where there is darkness, light; and where there is sadness, joy.
From the Prayer of Saint Francis

NOTE: Share reflections on how the saints have lived out the Beatitudes, Jesus' new commandment, and the theological virtues.

Reflection and Action

Words to Remember

Find and define the following.

Beatitudes Eight guidelines for true happiness given to us by Jesus.

new commandment (See page 93.)

virtue A habit of doing good.

Things to Think About

Can you think of a time when you thought something would bring you true happiness, and it did not? Why is that?

A famous Christian writer named Augustine wrote that we are restless until we look for real happiness with God. He said, "You have made us for Yourself, O Lord, and we are restless until we rest in You." Write in your journal what you think about his words.

Things to Share

Jesus' message of love was not one for those who were weak or afraid of life. Look what happened to Jesus after He preached and lived this message. Are you strong enough to love as Jesus did? How will you show this to others?

15 IN THE SERVICE OF OTHERS

How do you feel when you give or receive help?

Have you ever felt forgotten or alone?

EXPERIENCE: A Christian is someone who loves others as Jesus did and asks for nothing in return.

She could have lived a full life here in the United States, having what some might consider a privileged life, wanting for very little. But that was not the life Jean Donovan would live. Hers was to be a much more exciting adventure—the ultimate adventure.

As a lay missioner for the diocese of Cleveland, Jean worked in the Central American country of El Salvador. There with other missionaries she found some of the most satisfying moments that life could offer—working and ministering with the poor and sick in a land ravaged by war and political unrest. She and her fellow missioners were not interested in the politics of power. They traveled far from their own homeland to assist those who were powerless, the victims of political and economic forces beyond their control.

Certainly it was dangerous to be in El Salvador. But the needs of the people were greater and overcame any feelings of fear she may have had. As told in many newspaper reports and in two films entitled *Roses in December* and *Choices of the Heart*, Jean Donovan's life was brought to an abrupt end. On December 2, 1980, Jean Donovan and three other courageous women were martyred —killed not because they were weak, but because they were strong and determined in carrying out the work of Christian service. Jean Donovan's shining example has inspired many to follow on the same path of true adventure.

Do you think Jean Donovan's life was "ordinary" or "extraordinary"? Explain.

Why do you think Jean Donovan went to El Salvador? What was her source of strength to do what she did?

Why does the world need people like Jean Donovan? How is Jean Donovan an example for you?

NOTE: The photographs on these pages are of Jean Donovan, Sr. Maura Clarke, and Sr. Dorothy Kazel. Sr. Ita Ford was the fourth member of this group of martyrs.

1 We will be judged by our love.

STRESS the underlined copy.

Jesus' whole life was a shining example of service to others. "I am among you as one who serves" (Luke 22:27), He said. When we help others, we are following His example.

Once, when asked to sum up His teaching about how we should live, Jesus replied that we must love God and our neighbors as ourselves. To explain who that neighbor is, Jesus told the story of the Good Samaritan.

According to the story, a man who was on a journey was robbed, beaten, and left on the road to suffer. As he lay there, three people came along, but the first two passed by the suffering man. The third was a Samaritan, a hated enemy of the man who was robbed. The Samaritan stopped and dressed the man's wounds, took him to an inn, and even paid for his care!

DISCUSS: What does this parable mean?

After telling the story, Jesus asked, "In your opinion, which one of these three acted like a neighbor toward the man attacked by the robbers?" The answer came, "The one who was kind to him." Jesus said, "You go, then, and do the same" (from Luke 10:36–37).

Read the whole parable of the Good Samaritan in Luke 10:25–37.

From the Gospels we also learn about the right spirit with which we are to carry out our works of love. In Jesus' time, it was customary to put collection boxes outside the Temple area. The money left in these boxes was used to support the Temple and to aid the poor. One day Jesus used this custom to teach His followers about giving money to the poor.

As Jesus sat near the Temple treasury, he watched the people as they dropped in their money. Many rich men dropped in a lot of money; then a poor widow came along and dropped in two little copper coins, worth about a penny. He called his disciples together and said to them, "I tell you that this poor widow put more in the offering box than all the others. For the others put in what they had to spare of their riches

ASK: How could the widow have given "more" than the rich people?

but she, poor as she is, put in all she had— she gave all she had to live on."
Mark 12:41–44

At the end of our lives, how will we be judged for carrying out our Christian responsibilities? In describing the last judgment, Jesus tells why some will share in the joys of heaven and the others will not. To those who will be judged positively for their good works, Jesus will say:

I was hungry and you fed me, thirsty and you gave me a drink; I was a stranger and you received me in your homes, naked and you clothed me; I was sick and you took care of me, in prison and you visited me.
Matthew 25:35–36

Those being judged will ask Jesus when they did all of these things for Him, and He will reply, "I tell you, whenever you did this for one of the least important ones of mine, you did it for me!" (from Matthew 25:40).

We realize, then, that Jesus' instruction to love one another as He has loved us is at the heart of all Christian living. It is the joyful road each one of us must follow if we are to be counted as true followers of Jesus Christ. What do you think is the difference between the Good Samaritan and the poor widow?

Works of Mercy

Corporal Works

- Feed the hungry.
- Give drink to the thirsty.
- Clothe the naked.
- Help those imprisoned.
- Shelter the homeless.
- Care for the sick.
- Bury the dead.

Spiritual Works

- Share our knowledge with others.
- Give advice to those who need it.
- Comfort those who suffer.
- Be patient with others.
- Forgive those who hurt us.
- Give correction to those who need it.
- Pray for the living and the dead.

ASK: Who are the hungry, the thirsty, the sick, the stranger in your world right now?

2 We care for the physical and spiritual needs of others.

The Church is sent to announce the Good News of the Kingdom of God. This does not mean that the Church can simply talk about the Kingdom and remain unaware of the earthly needs of human beings. The Church teaches that we must take care of the *whole* person — physical needs as well as spiritual needs. These needs and our active Christlike response to them are expressed in the **Corporal and Spiritual Works of Mercy.**

By living the Works of Mercy, we put our faith into action, as Jesus has asked us. Where there has been a need in the past, Christian love has urged women and men to respond generously. Thus the Catholic Church has often been in the forefront of those seeking to establish justice for all and to offer comfort to those in need. In every community, we can see the Church involved in caring for the sick, the poor, and those with troubled lives.

Whether the needs are local or worldwide, the Catholic community is challenged by the Gospel to be a sign of the Kingdom of God by being involved in addressing these needs.

Though many problems seem to be impossible to solve completely, we know that we must work continually to establish true justice and peace.

The Church's official teaching reflects this central law of Christ — the law to love and serve. Even one of the pope's titles dramatizes this central law, for the pope is called "servant of the servants of God." This title brings home in a striking way the Christian idea of service.

During the last hundred years or so, statements of the popes have shown how much the Church is conscious of the actual conditions in which people live. At the end of the nineteenth century, Pope Leo XIII reminded politicians and governments that God had created all things for the use and happiness of all people. In more recent times, popes such as John XXIII, Paul VI, and John Paul II have challenged Christians to understand that the basis of all human society is to accept every individual as a *person*, possessing rights and duties. Again and again they have shown sensitivity to the poor and suffering. John Paul II has appealed for a greater sharing of the earth's riches to destroy the evils of disease, hunger, and poverty.

Hunger is one of the worst evils in the world. It has been said, "A hungry stomach cannot hear." What do you think that means? What can you do to help those who are in need of food?

NOTE: You might want to make or have the group make a poster or a bulletin board on the Laws of the Church. Display it; refer to it frequently.

3 Catholics have special laws to help live the Christian life.

Catholics also have another set of laws we use that remind us to live lives of love and service. They are called the **Laws of the Church**. These laws express some of the most important obligations we have as Catholics to grow in holiness and to share in the Church's works of service and **evangelization**, or sharing the Good News.

The Laws of the Church are usually summarized as follows:

1. Celebrate Christ's resurrection every Sunday (or Saturday evening) and on holy days of obligation by taking part in Mass and avoiding unnecessary work.

2. Lead a sacramental life. Receive Holy Communion frequently and the sacrament of Penance, or Reconciliation, regularly. We must receive Holy Communion at least once a year at Lent-Easter. We must confess within a year if we have committed serious, or mortal, sin.

3. Study Catholic teaching throughout life, especially in preparing for the sacraments.

4. Observe the marriage laws of the Church and give religious training to one's children.

5. Strengthen and support the Church: one's own parish, the worldwide Church, and the Holy Father.

6. Do penance, including not eating meat and fasting from food on certain days.

7. Join in the missionary work of the Church.

The Laws of the Church call us to a life of prayer and service. We cannot forget that, like all laws, these laws express the *minimum* that we must do to live our Catholic faith. We are called to build on these and to see them not just as obligations, but as reminders that our Catholic life is one of balance—a balance between our prayer and sacramental lives and the missionary efforts of the Church throughout the world. We accomplish all of this in our individual **parish** community, which is the focal point of the Christian life and where each assembly joins together with hundreds of millions of Catholics throughout the world.

Which of the Laws of the Church do you find most challenging? Why?

Do You Know

The Second Vatican Council described Christian service in this way: "In our times a special obligation binds us to make ourselves the neighbor of absolutely every person" (*Pastoral Constitution on the Church in the Modern World,* 27). This means that we must actively help people in need: the elderly, the abandoned, the hungry, and all those who seek justice and comfort.

ASSIGN for review and home study.

Church Teachings: Loving Service

- Jesus' instruction to love one another as He has loved us is at the heart of Christian living.

- The Corporal and Spiritual Works of Mercy include many of our active Christlike responses to the needs of others.

- Our Church, especially in the writings of our popes and bishops, encourages us to live lives of loving service, especially for the poor and those seeking justice.

Prayer

In your journal, reflect on the following words from Micah 6:8: "What the Lord requires of us is this: to do what is just, to show constant love, and to live in humble fellowship with our God."

Reflection and Action

Words to Remember

Find and define the following.

Works of Mercy Works done to relieve the physical and spiritual needs of others.

_____

evangelization The spreading, the sharing of the Good News of Jesus Christ.

_____

Laws of the Church Important obligations we have as Catholics to grow in holiness and service.

_____

Things to Think About

People are often surprised to learn of the many works of service accomplished by the Church. Think, for example, of the tremendous work done by Catholic Charities in every diocese. Our bishops' Campaign for Human Development has touched the lives of so many needy people. And many parishes seem to have a special outreach program. Are you aware of a particular program in your parish or one that you might suggest for your parish?

Things to Share

Think of all those who spend their lives in the service of others: single men and women, married couples, diocesan priests, religious priests, brothers, and sisters. How will you support their work and missionary efforts? What will you do today to prepare for your life of service?

16 LIFE EVERLASTING

Is there life after death?

Where do you turn for answers to this question?

The young king was dressed in his royal robes. Over his head he wore a mask of solid gold, and he lay stretched out, as if sleeping. But the king was not asleep; he was dead. He died over 1300 years before the time of Christ!

The young king's name was Tutankhamen. He was buried, as were the kings of Egypt, in a tomb that was specially constructed for him during his life. But the tomb of an Egyptian king was not just a burial place. It was a sort of halfway station to the next world. For the Egyptians were firm believers that there was a world to come after death. They also believed that the deceased person would have to travel to get to that world.

To help the king make his journey, the tomb was filled with the things he had loved in this world and might need for his comfort in the next. These things might include chairs, beds, and other furniture, perfumes, clothing, chariots, boats—and even food!

In 1922 when the tomb of Tutankhamen was discovered, it yielded riches almost beyond description. Gold, silver, precious stones, and objects crafted with exquisite care were in abundance. These objects can be seen today in the Cairo Museum in Egypt. They attest to the strong belief of the ancient Egyptians in life after death.

Why do you think the Egyptians and other ancient peoples took so much care in constructing tombs for the dead?

(Discuss why we have a reverence today for the body of the

deceased.)

Imagine yourself to be an ancient Egyptian king or queen. What objects would you want to have with you on a journey into the next world? Why?

(Invite the young people to share their responses.)

1 The mystery of death is answered in the resurrection of Jesus Christ.

STRESS the underlined copy.

Strange as it may seem, death is the greatest mystery of life. Down through the ages, it has haunted and puzzled men and women everywhere.

In early Old Testament times, people were not sure about life after death. They had some vague notion that men and women lived on through their children. That is why the aged and childless Abraham and Sarah were so overjoyed when they heard that they would have a son, Isaac. They believed that parents, by passing on their heritage, would continue to live in their offspring.

Centuries later, however, death still remained a mystery. In later Old Testament times, the ancient Jews considered life after death as some kind of vague existence. For this reason, they believed that the greatest gift they could receive from God was to live a long life.

In the time of Jesus, two opposite opinions were held about life after death. Some Jews believed there was no life after death; others had a growing understanding of an afterlife and believed in life after death.

Jesus Himself left no doubt as to His own teaching on life after death. Speaking to those who denied the resurrection of the dead, Jesus said, "You are completely wrong!" (Mark 12:27). He told them that God promised life, not death, and explained that life after death is different from our human experience.

Belief in **resurrection** was accepted by everyone in the early Church. It was so central to the faith of early Christians that Paul wrote, "If there is no resurrection of the dead, Christ himself has not been raised. And if Christ has not been raised, our preaching is empty of content and your faith is empty, too" (from 1 Corinthians 15:13–14).

With this hope and faith in Christ's resurrection, the Christian community could endure persecution and suffering. Their faith was not shaken by rejection and ridicule. Even though Christians loved and cherished the gift of life as Jesus did, they also knew that dying for their faith was a sharing in the redemptive death of Christ. Christ had conquered death. They would rise to new life in the risen Lord.

Jesus was unique and extraordinary in His life and death. He died on the cross, but He was raised to new life by His Father! We believe that because of Christ's resurrection, we will rise to new life after death. For the Christian, death is not the final chapter in life.

What does it mean for you to share in Christ's resurrection?

NOTE: Explore with the young people any fears or problems they may have concerning death.

Do You Know

Some early Christians asked Paul how the dead were to be raised and what kind of "body" they would have. He called their questions nonsensical and said that in the "twinkling of an eye" our earthly bodies would be transformed into spiritual ones. Paul said, "What no one ever saw or heard, what no one ever thought could happen, is the very thing God prepared for those who love God" (from 1 Corinthians 2:9).

104

DISCUSS: How does the Christian view of death affect your feelings about death?

2 Catholics believe in life everlasting.

Each week the Church professes its belief in the resurrection of the body with these words from the Nicene Creed: "We look for the resurrection of the dead and the life of the world to come." In the Apostles' Creed we say, "I believe in the resurrection of the body and life everlasting." These statements of faith, or **creeds**, leave no doubt as to the teaching of the Catholic Church about death and resurrection.

Catholics believe that when a person dies, life is not ended but changed. In the Mass of Christian Burial the hopeful, consoling words of John's Gospel are often proclaimed. According to that Gospel, Jesus' friend Lazarus had died. Lazarus' sister Martha, in her grief, heard these beautiful words from Jesus: "Your brother will rise to life." Then Jesus continued: "I am the resurrection and the life. Whoever believes in me will live, even though that person dies; and whoever lives and believes in me will never die." From John 11:17–27.

In the important moments of Christian life—from birth to death—the Church community supports and guides its members. At the moment of death, we are judged in relation to how well we loved and served God and others. The **general judgment** before God on the last day will affirm before all the world whether we chose to love or not to love.

For those who have followed God's way and have served Christ in others, death will be the beginning of endless peace and happiness. This is **heaven**—everlasting union with God. For many, however, there will be a process of purification needed because of our sins. This process is called **purgatory**. Yet, those experiencing purgatory are certain of heaven. Our Church reminds us not to forget those who have died but always to remember them in our prayers, especially at Mass.

A very different beginning awaits those who have wasted their gift of God's life. They refused to follow God's way, to recognize or serve Christ in others. Instead they freely chose a life of sin and selfishness. They had no intention of being sorry or of changing their ways. For them there is nothing ahead but eternal misery. This is **hell**—everlasting separation from God.

The Church believes and teaches that no one is condemned to hell without freely deciding to reject God and God's love. We ourselves turn away from God's mercy. God never turns away from us. God wills that every person born should be saved and share eternal life.

Share your thoughts on the following statement: We do not judge others; God alone is the just and merciful judge.

105

Mary is the greatest of the saints.

Just as God chose us to be followers of Christ, God chose Mary to be the mother of the Savior, the Word made flesh. She did not hesitate to say yes to God's call to be the mother of Jesus, the Son of God and our Brother.

As a faithful daughter of Israel, Mary reflected on God's word and carried it out in her life. She gave birth to Jesus, dedicated her life to Him, and was present at His crucifixion. On the day of Pentecost, Mary was also there, praying with the other disciples as they waited for the coming of the Holy Spirit. She really could be considered Christ's first disciple, the one who heard the Good News of God's love in the world and who acted on it.

In John's Gospel we learn something more about Mary and her relationship to us. According to this Gospel, as Jesus was hanging on the cross He saw His mother and the beloved disciple. Jesus said to His mother, "He is your son." Then to the disciple He said, "She is your mother" (John 19:26–27). This passage helps us to understand that Mary is our Mother, too. Not only is she the **Mother of God**, she is the Mother of all who follow Jesus Christ.

During the year, we celebrate many feasts to honor Mary. It seems as if every culture has a special title for her. Yet she is more to us than a devotional figure, distant and seemingly removed from our everyday experiences. Mary was a real human being. She was blessed by God to be full of grace. But this did not keep her from life's struggles and joys.

NOTE: If time allows, have the group do a gospel search to "discover" Mary. Use Luke 1:39–56, Luke 2:4–19, Luke 2:41–52, John 2:1–12, John 19:25–27.

ASK: What prayer do we pray to Mary?

For almost 2000 years, our Church has been blessed with the holy lives of men and women who have accepted the challenge to live the message of Christ. They are our heroes and heroines in faith and have come from all walks of life. Some have been kings and queens; some have been poor and needy; most have lived lives just like we do. But all have responded to God's love and shared that love with others. They have lived according to God's way. These are the **saints**, and we are brothers and sisters with them, especially when we follow the path to holiness. We believe that all those who have gone before us, who are now with God, continue to pray for us and for our good. That is what we call the **communion of saints**.

When will you take time to be with Mary and the saints in prayer?

Church Teachings About "Last Things"

- The "last things" is a term that refers to death, judgment, purgatory, heaven, and hell.

- God wishes for all people to be saved and to live forever with God in heaven.

- Those who are not saved have freely chosen to separate themselves from God.

- Mary is the greatest of the saints. We believe she was free from original sin from the first moment of her life. This belief is called the **Immaculate Conception**.

- We believe that, at the end of her life, the Blessed Virgin Mary was taken body and soul to heaven. This belief is called the **Assumption**.

Prayer

Loving God, some people think that heaven is flying around with angels and saints all day. If that were true, I would rather have my life just as it is. But I know that the truth and inexpressible joy of heaven, being with You forever, starts here and now. Help me to choose Your way of love. Help me to begin today. Amen.

Reflection and Action

Words to Remember

Find and define the following.

heaven Everlasting union with God.

_____

_____

hell Everlasting separation from God.

_____

_____

purgatory A process of purification due to sin.

_____

_____

Things to Think About

Life is, in a sense, a preparation for death. Yet we do not give all our time to thoughts of death and dying. Every day we are continuously involved in *living*. Our relationship with God and others continues to develop and grow. Our life after death will be, in a sense, a further development of those relationships. Doing well what we must do is the best way of preparing for death. This means listening to God in prayer and being open to doing what is loving for others as we meet Christ in our daily lives.

Things to Share

People need to hear that our real preparation for the unknown day of death takes on special meaning right now. With confidence in Jesus, we need to take a chance on life — truly live. Jesus has set up the standard. The real judgment of our lives will be how well we have performed in love and service to God and others. When will you share the message of life everlasting?

Unit 4 Test

A. Write the term next to the definition that matches it.

The Beatitudes	Resurrection
The Laws of the Church	The Ten Commandments
The Law of Love	Corporal Works of Mercy
Covenant	Evangelization
Virtue	Moses
Faith	Hope
Heaven	Spiritual Works of Mercy
Love	

1. *Corporal Works of Mercy* _____ are the works Christians are called to do to relieve the physical needs of others.

2. *The Laws of the Church* _____ express the most important obligations we have as Catholics to grow in holiness in the Church.

3. *Evangelization* _____ means sharing the Good News of the Gospel with those who have not yet heard it.

4. *The Beatitudes* _____ are eight guidelines for true happiness given us by Jesus.

5. *Moses* _____ was the leader of the Israelites to whom God gave the Ten Commandments.

6. *Covenant* _____ is a special agreement between God and people.

7. *The Ten Commandments* _____ are the laws of the covenant that summarized the responsibilities the people would have toward God.

8. *Resurrection* _____ means rising to new life after death.

9. *The Law of love* _____ is the most important of all the commandments because it tells us we must love God above all others, and love our neighbor as we love ourselves.

10. *Spiritual Works of Mercy* _____ are works Christians are called to do to relieve the spiritual needs of others.

11. *Virtue* _____ is the name given to a habit of doing good.

12. *Heaven* _____ refers to the state of everlasting union with God.

13. *Love* _____ is the virtue that draws us into the closest relationship we can have with God.

14. *Hope* _____ is the virtue that helps us to trust in God even when things are going badly.

15. *Faith* _____ is the virtue that helps us to believe and to accept all that God teaches and reveals to us.

B. Circle the letter beside the response that does *not* belong.

1. God made a covenant with the Israelites so that they could
   - a. have plenty to eat.
   - b. be free from slavery in Egypt.
   - c. be free from the slavery of sin.
   - d. live as faithful people.

2. The theological virtues are
   - a. hope.
   - b. love.
   - c. courage.
   - d. faith.

108

3. Jesus taught His disciples about love. He said,

   a. love even your enemies.

   b. pray for those who persecute you.

   c. love one another as I have loved you.

   (d.) think of yourself first.

4. Jesus taught that at the end of life we will be judged on

   (a.) our power.

   b. our love.

   c. our service for others.

   d. our willingness to see Him in others.

5. Catholics believe that when we die

   a. life is changed, not ended.

   (b.) we live on only in our children.

   c. the body is resurrected to life everlasting.

   d. death will be the beginning of endless happiness.

C. Respond as thoughtfully and completely as possible.

1. Good laws help us to be free. Explain.

   (Accept appropriate responses.)

   _____

   _____

   _____

2. Jesus' new commandment might sound simple, but it demands strength and courage. Explain.

   Jesus loved us to the point of giving this life for us. It is very

   difficult to love others this way.

   _____

   _____

3. Recall the story of the Good Samaritan. What important lesson was Jesus teaching in this story?

   That every person, regardless of race, religion, or nationality,

   is our neighbor.

   _____

   _____

4. Describe two works of mercy that you are able to do in your life right now.

   (Accept appropriate responses.)

   _____

   _____

   _____

5. Why do you think Mary is considered the first of all Jesus' disciples?

   Responses should include: Mary is His Mother; she

   dedicated her life to Him; she was present at His crucifixion.

   _____

   _____

Semester 2 Test

A. Choose the correct term to complete each statement.

The Eucharist   Transubstantiation

The Liturgy   The Last Supper

Reconciliation   The Mass

Social sin   Conscience

Absolution   Venial sin

Confession   The Immaculate Conception

The Assumption

The "last things"   The communion of saints

1. *The Assumption* _____ is the belief that Mary was taken body and soul into heaven.

2. *The Communion of Saints* _____ is the belief that all those who are now with God continue to pray for us and we for and to them.

3. *The Last Supper* _____ was the Passover meal at which Jesus gave us the Eucharist.

4. *Conscience* _____ is the ability we have to judge whether an action is right or wrong.

5. *Reconciliation* _____ is the sacrament in which our sins are forgiven and we are reconciled to God, the Church, and to one another.

6. *Venial sin* _____ is a sin, but less serious than mortal sin.

7. *The Liturgy* _____ is the name given to the official public worship of the Church.

8. *Social sin* _____ is a sinful choice of society, such as prejudice of any kind.

9. *The Immaculate Conception* _____ is the belief that Mary was free from original sin from the first moment of her life.

10. *Absolution* _____ is the sign of God's forgiveness that the priest gives us in the sacrament of Reconciliation.

11. *The Eucharist* _____ is the sacrament of the Body and Blood of Christ.

12. *Transubstantiation* _____ is the name given to the changing of the bread and wine into the Body and Blood of Christ.

13. *Confession* _____ is the telling of one's sins to a priest in the sacrament of Reconciliation.

14. *The Mass* _____ is our celebration of the Eucharist. It comes from a Latin word meaning "sent out."

15. *The "last things"* _____ is a term that refers to death, judgment, purgatory, heaven, and hell.

B. Circle the letter beside the correct response.

1. The commandment that teaches us to respect the sacredness of life is

    a. the eighth commandment.

    (b.) the fifth commandment.

    c. the fourth commandment.

    d. the first commandment.

2. The commandment that teaches us to respect the good name of others and to be honest is

    a. the first commandment.

    b. the ninth commandment.

    c. the sixth commandment.

    (d.) the eighth commandment.

3. The commandment that teaches us to honor God's name and to show special reverence for the name of Jesus Christ is

   (a.) the second commandment.

   b. the fourth commandment.

   c. the tenth commandment.

   d. the third commandment.

4. The Church teaches us that

   a. God condemns sinners to hell.

   b. God turns away from us when we sin.

   c. God will judge us on how successful we have been.

   (d.) God wills that everyone should have eternal life.

5. The Church tells us that Mary

   a. was divine, not human.

   (b.) is the Mother of God and our Mother, too.

   c. was kept by God from life's struggles.

   d. was not present at the crucifixion.

C. **Answer as completely and thoughtfully as possible.**

1. As Christians we believe that we share in Christ's resurrection. What does that mean to you?

   That we, too, will rise from death to new life.

2. As followers of Jesus Christ we are called to serve others in His name. How can someone your age do this?

   (Accept appropriate responses.)

3. Mortal sin is the most serious sin against God. What three conditions make a sin mortal?

   The sin must do serious harm to our relationship with God

   and others; we must have clear knowledge; we must freely

   choose to do it.

4. As Catholics we are challenged by the needs of people in our world. Tell about one of these needs that you would like to do something about, and why.

   (Accept appropriate responses.)

5. You have finished this book *One Faith, One Lord*. Explain *one* thing you have learned that will help you be a better follower of Jesus Christ.

   (Encourage the young people to be candid and thoughtful.)

For Better Understanding

Faith Summary

The following are brief summary statements meant to help you review what you know and believe as a Catholic.

1. Prayer is important in life.

It is important that some prayers be known and said frequently, so that people can pray, not only alone, but also together as a community. These prayers include the Sign of the Cross, the Our Father, the Hail Mary, the Glory to the Father, the Apostles' Creed, an Act of Contrition, and the Rosary. It is also important to talk with God spontaneously and informally, and to listen to and reflect on God's word. These are some of the different forms of prayer we share.

2. Participating in the Liturgy is important.

As members of the Christian community, we are privileged to participate in the liturgical (or official) prayer of the Church, especially in the Eucharist. We can also share in the Liturgy of the Hours, particularly Morning and Evening Prayer.

3. Being familiar with the Bible is important.

Reading the Bible is in itself a form of prayer. The authors of the Bible were inspired by God. Together with tradition the Bible is the primary source of Church teaching. The Bible is a collection of divinely inspired books with different human authors, histories, and types of literature. "All Scripture is inspired by God and is useful for teaching the truth, rebuking error, correcting faults, and giving instruction for right living" (2 Timothy 3:16).

4. The Trinity is the Mystery of the one God in three divine Persons—Father, Son, Holy Spirit.

From the Old Testament we know that God is revealed as the one, true, personal God. Over many centuries, God prepared people for the revelation of the Trinity. In the fullness of time, Jesus more fully revealed the Father, the First Person of the Blessed Trinity; revealed Himself as the divine Son of God, the Second Person of the Trinity; and made known the Holy Spirit, the Third Person of the Trinity.

5. All are called to worship God.

All people are called to worship the living God, who is eternal, holy, just, merciful, infinitely wise, and perfect. This worship is accomplished especially by carrying out God's will in everything we say and do and by using the talents God has given us as best we can.

6. We are called to witness to our Christian love.

As believers we are called to give public witness to our faith and personal love of God in the way we live our lives. Our faith in God and union with Christ entail an obligation to work at solving the problems and troubles in our own world here and now.

7. God is the Creator of the universe.

When we say that the entire universe was created by God out of nothing, we are not denying the scientific theory of evolution. Church teachings are not in conflict but in harmony with science. When Christians consider the doctrine of creation, we also remember God's continuing activity in working out the salvation of the world. God is actively and lovingly present in human history from start to finish. God will bring this saving work to completion only at the end of the world when there will be "a new heaven and a new earth."

8. Jesus Christ is the Son of God.

The Incarnation—the taking on of human flesh by the Second Person of the Trinity—is the greatest of God's works. Jesus came on earth and entered human history, renewed the world, and gave eternal life to all.

9. Jesus Christ is true God and true Man; He is the Savior and Redeemer.

As a man, Jesus thought with a human mind, acted with a human will, and loved with a human heart. He joined Himself with every human being, except in sin. Jesus is also truly divine. He is not only fully human, but the Son of God. All of us were called to salvation by His obedience to the will of His Father. Out of love for His Father and love of us, He gave Himself up to death, and passed through death to the glory of His Father. By His death and resurrection, Jesus redeemed humankind from sin.

10. The Holy Spirit carries out Christ's work in the world.

Jesus promised to send the Holy Spirit, the Paraclete, to be with us and remain with us forever. The Holy Spirit, the Third Person of the Blessed Trinity, did come at Pentecost and is present in a special way in the community of the Church. When we answer the invitation to love God and one another, the Spirit is at work.

11. The sacraments are actions of Christ in the Church.

The sacraments are effective signs of Jesus' presence in our community. They are not ordinary signs because they cause to happen what they signify. They give us a share in God's life and blessings. In the sacraments we meet Jesus Christ, who shares God's own life of grace with us. Each sacrament marks a particular time of growth as a Christian and invites us to share in God's life in a special way.

12. There are seven sacraments.

Baptism is the sacrament of rebirth. In receiving Baptism, we are united with Jesus in His death and resurrection, cleansed from original sin and personal sins, welcomed into the community of the Church, and more closely related to God.

Confirmation is the sacrament by which baptized persons are sealed with the Gift of the Holy Spirit. It is linked with the other two Sacraments of Initiation, Baptism and the Eucharist. In celebrating Confirmation, we ask for the grace needed to live a mature Christian life and to deepen our faith.

The Eucharist is the center of sacramental life and is primary among the sacraments. We celebrate the Eucharist in obedience to Jesus' instruction at the Last Supper: "Do this in memory of me." When the priest consecrates bread and wine, they become the Body and Blood of Christ. Christ Himself is really present, sacramentally, under the appearances of bread and wine. In the Mass the death and resurrection of Jesus are celebrated and renewed. The Eucharist is also a meal that recalls the Last Supper, celebrates our unity in Christ, and anticipates the messianic banquet of the Kingdom. In the meal, Jesus nourishes us with the Bread of Life, His own Self, and unites us more closely with God and with one another. A Christian must be in the state of grace to receive the Eucharist worthily.

Penance, or Reconciliation, is the sacrament by which Catholics celebrate God's merciful forgiveness for sins committed after Baptism. After a sincere confession of sin, true sorrow, and resolution not to sin again, we receive absolution as a means of reconciliation with God and the community. In Penance Catholics are also reconciled with the Church. Although perfect sorrow, or contrition, restores a sinner to grace, sacramental confession is the ordinary way for serious sinners to be reconciled with Christ and the Church.

The Anointing of the Sick is the sacrament for the seriously ill, the infirm, the aged, and the dying. In this sacrament the Church carries on the healing and forgiving ministry of Jesus Christ, who often visited and healed the sick. The Church's message of hope and comfort is reflected in these words taken from a prayer that can be used during the rite of anointing: "Look with compassion upon your servant N., whom we have anointed in your name with this holy oil for the healing of his/her body and spirit."

Matrimony is the sacrament through which God blesses the love between a husband and wife so that they may love each other all their lives. The married couple receives special graces to help them direct their family in loving relationships and toward full participation in the Christian community.

Holy Orders is the sacrament by which men are ordained and given special powers and responsibilities for the Church. They are put in positions of special service for the building up of the Body of Christ. Those who become bishops, priests, and deacons receive this sacrament.

13. The Holy Spirit urges us to live a new way of life.

The Holy Spirit urges us to seek what is good and to grow in virtues such as charity, joy, peace, patience, kindness, goodness, humility, fidelity, modesty, continence, and chastity. God's plan for us is that, united with Jesus, we give a free answer to God's call. Our human nature has been badly impaired by original sin, which is transmitted to all. The weakness resulting from original sin is overcome by grace.

The greatest difficulty we face in reaching salvation is sin. Personal sin, which is sin committed by an individual acting knowingly and deliberately, violates the moral law. Sin is freely choosing to do what we know is wrong, disobeying God's law on purpose. Christians must have clear knowledge of what is right and wrong so they can choose, with an informed conscience, to love God and live the Gospel.

14. Christians are called to live a moral life.

Christian morality defines a way of living that is worthy of a human being and a child of God. We grow and respond positively to God by maturing in the new life Jesus gives us.

Each Christian must have a right conscience and follow it. Conscience is not a feeling, but a personal judgment that something is right or wrong because of the will and law of God. As Catholic Christians we must respond to the teaching authority of the Church. Some moral values are absolute and must never be disregarded. We are called to faithful observance of the Ten Commandments, the Law of Love, the Laws of the Church, and just civil laws. The center of morality is love of God.

As Catholics sustained by faith, we are able to live a life of love of God and one another. There are certain responsibilities and obligations flowing from this love. The specifics of our morality, which we must apply to current problems, must be understood and applied within guidelines (for example, the Commandments, the Sermon on the Mount, as well as the Spiritual and Corporal Works of Mercy). As Christians we have specific moral obligations toward God, toward other people, and toward ourselves. As Christians we are called to form a right conscience, choose what is right, avoid sin and the occasions of sin, and live our lives according to the spirit of love.

15. The Church is the People of God.

With His disciples, Jesus formed the community we call Church. This is the special name for those who call themselves Christians and follow the way of Jesus, rooted in beliefs and traditions that go back through the centuries to the apostles. In the New Testament, the Church is beautifully described as the People of God. Catholics believe that the Church was founded on Christ with Peter and the apostles as its first leaders and teachers. Their authority and call to service has been handed down to their successors, the Pope and bishops of the Catholic Church. The members of the Church have different gifts and responsibilities, but all are called to holiness and service.

16. Mary is the Mother of God and Mother of the Church.

Our Blessed Mother has a very special place in the history of salvation and in the Church. Mary, the ever-virgin Mother of Jesus, is very close to us as our spiritual Mother. In addition to receiving the special gift of being Mother of God, she has been preserved from all stain of original sin (her Immaculate Conception) and has been assumed body and soul to heaven (her Assumption). Special veneration is due her.

Christians honor the other saints in heaven and are challenged by the example of their lives. In addition we honor, respect, and pray for all of the faithful departed.

Because of our belief in the resurrection and eternal life, Catholics consider all those who share in God's life through grace, whether they are now living or have died, to be part of one community in Christ. We call this community the Communion of Saints. Together we are witnesses to the Gospel and members of the one Body of Christ.

17. Our call is to final reunion with God.

When Christ returns as judge of the living and dead to bring history to its appointed end and hands over His people to the Father, "he will change our weak mortal bodies and make them like his own glorious body, using that power by which he is able to bring all things under his rule" (Philippians 3:21).

Since each of us will be judged after death, we share the awesome responsibility for our own eternal destiny.

We all have reason to live and to face death with courage, hope, and joy, because the Lord's resurrection means that death has been conquered. On the day of the last judgment all will reach their eternal destiny, and those who have done right shall live a life of eternal happiness with God.

Helps to Understanding the Bible

- The Bible is like a small library; it is a collection of seventy-three smaller books.

- The Bible has two main parts: the Old Testament, which contains forty-six books about the faith relationship between God and the Israelites, later called the Jews; and the New Testament, which contains twenty-seven books about Jesus Christ, His message, and His first followers.

- The Bible has many different forms and styles of writing, including poetry, history, laws, parables, wise sayings, fables, hymns, family trees, and short stories.

- We refer to the writings of the Bible as God's word because it was inspired by God.

- Because the Bible was written so long ago and in so many different styles of writing, we need to take time to study it carefully. Knowing the background of the human authors, the culture of the times, and the different forms and styles of writing permit us to better understand God's word.

- The Bible is a book about faith. It cannot be read like a science book or modern history book.

- The Bible should be read reverently and with a mind and heart open to its meaning for our lives.

The Seven Sacraments

Sacraments We Celebrate	Signs We See	Signs We Hear	Why We Celebrate
Baptism	pouring of water	I baptize you.	Jesus shares God's life of grace with a person.
Confirmation	bishop anointing	Be sealed with the Gift of the Holy Spirit.	Jesus sends the Holy Spirit to strengthen those confirmed.
Eucharist	bread and wine	This is My Body. This is My Blood.	Jesus shares His Body and Blood with us.
Reconciliation	priest makes the sign of the cross	I absolve you from your sins . . .	Jesus forgives those who are sorry.
Anointing of the Sick	priest anoints sick person	Through this holy anointing ... may the Lord save you and raise you up.	Jesus comforts and strengthens those who are sick.
Matrimony	joining of hands	I take you to be my wife (or husband).	Jesus blesses the love of a man and a woman.
Holy Orders	bishop lays his hands on head of person being ordained.	A special prayer of consecration	Jesus sends us bishops, priests, and deacons to help us carry out His mission.

The Liturgical Year

As the Second Vatican Council reminded us, the Church is a great mystery of God's love in and for the world. The events of the past marked by God's love and care for us become signs of the mysteries of grace and salvation. We use the word *mystery* because we know we can never completely understand the deep meaning of these spiritual realities. The more we know about God's love and the ways it is shown to us, the more we realize our inability to fully express its depth and meaning for us.

By remembering and celebrating important events and people whom we revere as saints in the long history of God's relationship with humankind, we can come closer to a better understanding of that relationship. At the same time we are challenged to express to others, through our own Christian lifestyle, the importance of God's life in us as individuals and as a community.

The liturgy is the Church's official means of celebrating our tradition, our experience of God's love and salvation. Our liturgy, or community worship, consists of the celebration of Mass and the other sacraments. It also includes the special prayers of the Church called the Liturgy of the Hours.

This special section of *One Faith, One Lord* contains brief outlines concerning how and when the Church celebrates our liturgical life. Taken together these events and celebrations make up the liturgical year, or calendar of feasts and seasons. Ours is a long and rich tradition with a great deal to celebrate.

Advent

Advent is the beginning of our liturgical year. It is the time of preparation for the coming of God's Kingdom and for Christmas. We remember the long period of waiting for the Messiah by the people of Israel. We celebrate God's messages of hope through the prophets, and Mary's and Joseph's faithfulness to God's plan. The central figures in Advent are the prophets, John the Baptist, Mary and Joseph, and the Holy Spirit.

The Advent season begins four Sundays before December 25 and ends at the Christmas Vigil Mass. The color of the vestments and decorations for the days of Advent is traditionally violet. It signifies that this is a time of expectation.

Some important feast days celebrated during Advent are:

St. Francis Xavier	Dec. 3
St. Ambrose	Dec. 7
Immaculate Conception	Dec. 8
Our Lady of Guadalupe	Dec. 12
St. John of the Cross	Dec. 14

● What other feasts do you celebrate in this season?

Christmas

Christmas is, of course, our celebration of Jesus' birth and the joyous events that are associated with it. Jesus is the Word of God made flesh, the awaited Messiah. The central figures we remember at this time are Jesus, Mary, Joseph, and John the Baptist.

The Christmas season begins at the vigil Mass on Christmas Eve and ends on the feast of the Baptism of the Lord. Thus it takes in the period from Jesus' birth to the beginning of His public ministry. The color of the vestments for this season is white. You may also see gold vestments and decorations. This is to symbolize our joy at the presence of Christ.

Some important feast days during the Christmas season are:

Christmas	Dec. 25
Holy Family—usually the Sunday after Christmas	
St. Stephen	Dec. 26
St. John, Apostle and Evangelist	Dec. 27
Holy Innocents	Dec. 28
Mary, Mother of God	Jan. 1
St. Elizabeth Seton	Jan. 4
St. John Neumann	Jan. 5
Epiphany—the Sunday between Jan. 2 and Jan. 8	
Baptism of the Lord—the Sunday after Epiphany	

● What other feasts do you celebrate in this season?

Lent

Lent is the time of preparation for Easter, the greatest feast of the Church. During Lent we are asked to concentrate on reforming our lives through positive acts of Christian love and through prayer and penance. It is a very important time of spiritual preparation for those seeking Baptism and for the whole parish. In this season, we try to become more like Christ in His love for God and others by His dying and rising to new life. The central figures in the readings for this season are Jesus, the disciples, and the prophets.

The season of Lent begins on Ash Wednesday, forty days before Easter, and ends on Thursday of Holy Week. The predominant liturgical color is violet, symbolic of penance and reflection. In your parish there may be an emphasis on the sacrament of Reconciliation during Lent as a further means of entering into the spirit of the season.

Some important feasts during the Lenten season are:

St. Patrick	Mar. 17
St. Joseph, Husband of Mary	Mar. 19
Annunciation	Mar. 25

● What other feasts do you celebrate in this season?

The Easter Triduum

Lent concludes on Thursday of Holy Week. Then the Church remembers the death and resurrection of Jesus during the Easter Triduum. These three days are the most important time of the Church year. The Triduum begins on Holy Thursday with the evening Mass of the Lord's Supper, is continued through Good Friday with the celebration of the passion of the Lord and Holy Saturday, to reach its high point in the Easter Vigil, and concludes with Vespers (evening prayer) of Easter Sunday.

The Easter Season

During the Easter season we celebrate the resurrection and ascension of Jesus and the coming of the Holy Spirit at Pentecost. The central figures in the readings are Jesus, the apostles, the Holy Spirit, and the leaders of the early Church. The predominant color for vestments is white, signifying the joy of the season. Gold may be used on some feasts, especially Easter and the Ascension, and red on the feast of Pentecost. Important feasts celebrated during Eastertime are:

St. Anselm	April 21
St. Mark	April 25
St. Catherine of Siena	April 29
St. Joseph the Worker	May 1

• What other feasts do you celebrate in this season?

Ordinary Time

All of the other Sundays of the year are known as Sundays during Ordinary Time. The emphasis on these Sundays is on the celebration of and instruction in our Christian faith and morals. The periods of Ordinary Time occur between the Christmas and Lenten seasons, and after the Easter season until the beginning of Advent. The last Sunday of the year is the feast of Christ the King. The liturgical color for Ordinary Time is green, a sign of hope.

Some important feasts we celebrate in ordinary time are:

St. Francis de Sales	Jan. 24
Conversion of Paul, Apostle	Jan. 25
St. Thomas Aquinas	Jan. 28
St. John Bosco	Jan. 31
Presentation of the Lord	Feb. 2
Our Lady of Lourdes	Feb. 11
Bl. Katharine Drexel	Mar. 3
Sts. John Fisher and Thomas More	June 22
Birth of John the Baptist	June 24
Sts. Peter and Paul	June 29
Bl. Junípero Serra	July 1
St. Benedict	July 11
Bl. Kateri Tekakwitha	July 14
St. Bonaventure	July 15
Sts. Joachim and Ann	July 26
St. Ignatius of Loyola	July 31
Transfiguration	Aug. 6
St. Dominic	Aug. 8
St. Clare	Aug. 11
Assumption	Aug. 15
St. Augustine	Aug. 28
Birth of Mary	Sept. 8
St. Peter Claver	Sept. 9
St. Matthew	Sept. 21
St. Vincent De Paul	Sept. 27
St. Francis Assisi	Oct. 4
St. Luke	Oct. 18
Sts. Isaac Jogues and John de Brebeuf	Oct. 19
All Saints Day	Nov. 1
All Souls Day	Nov. 2
St. Martin de Porres	Nov. 3
St. Francis Xavier Cabrini	Nov. 13
St. Rose Philippine Duchesne	Nov. 18

• What other feasts do you celebrate in this season?

Prayers and Practices

Sign of the Cross

In the name of the Father,
and of the Son,
and of the Holy Spirit. Amen.

Glory to the Father

Glory to the Father,
and to the Son,
and to the Holy Spirit.
As it was in the beginning,
is now, and will be forever. Amen.

Apostles' Creed

I believe in God, the Father almighty,
creator of heaven and earth.

I believe in Jesus Christ,
his only Son, our Lord.
He was conceived by the power
of the Holy Spirit
and born of the Virgin Mary.
He suffered under Pontius Pilate,
was crucified, died, and was buried.
He descended to the dead.
On the third day he rose again.
He ascended into heaven,
and is seated at the right hand
of the Father.
He will come again to judge
the living and the dead.

I believe in the Holy Spirit,
the holy catholic Church,
the communion of saints,
the forgiveness of sins,
the resurrection of the body,
and the life everlasting. Amen.

Nicene Creed

We believe in one God,
the Father, the Almighty,
maker of heaven and earth,
of all that is seen and unseen.

We believe in one Lord, Jesus Christ,
the only Son of God,
eternally begotten of the Father,
God from God, Light from Light,
true God from true God,
begotten, not made,
one in Being with the Father.
Through him all things were made.
For us men and for our salvation
he came down from heaven:
by the power of the Holy Spirit
he was born of the Virgin Mary,
and became man.

For our sake he was crucified
under Pontius Pilate;
he suffered, died, and was buried.
On the third day he rose again
in fulfillment of the Scriptures;
he ascended into heaven and is seated
at the right hand of the Father.
He will come again in glory
to judge the living and the dead,
and his kingdom will have no end.

We believe in the Holy Spirit,
the Lord, the giver of life,
who proceeds from the Father
and the Son.
With the Father and the Son
he is worshiped and glorified.
He has spoken through the Prophets.

We believe in one holy catholic
and apostolic Church.
We acknowledge one baptism
for the forgiveness of sins.
We look for the resurrection of the dead,
and the life of the world to come. Amen.

Our Father

Our Father, who art in heaven,
hallowed be thy name;
thy kingdom come;
thy will be done on earth
as it is in heaven.
Give us this day our daily bread;
and forgive us our trepasses
as we forgive those
who trespass against us;
and lead us not into temptation,
but deliver us from evil. Amen.

Hail Mary

Hail Mary, full of grace,
the Lord is with you;
blessed are you among women,
and blessed is the fruit
of your womb, Jesus.
Holy Mary, Mother of God,
pray for us sinners now
and at the hour of our death. Amen.

Morning Offering

My God, I offer you all my prayers, works,
and sufferings of this day for all the
intentions of your most Sacred Heart. Amen.

Evening Prayer

Dear God,
before I sleep
I want to thank you for this day,
so full of your kindness
and your joy.
I close my eyes to rest
safe in your loving care.

Grace Before Meals

Bless us, O Lord,
and these your gifts
which we are about to receive
from your bounty,
through Christ our Lord. Amen.

Grace After Meals

We give you thanks, almighty God,
for these and all your gifts
which we have received
through Christ our Lord. Amen.

Memorare

Remember, O most gracious Virgin Mary, that
never was it known that anyone who fled to
your protection, implored your help, or sought
your intercession was left unaided. Inspired with
this confidence, we fly unto you, O Virgin of
virgins, our Mother. To you we come, before
you we kneel, sinful and sorrowful. O Mother of
the Word made flesh, do not despise our
petitions, but in your mercy hear and answer
them. Amen.

Act of Contrition

My God,
I am sorry for my sins with all my heart.
In choosing to do wrong
and failing to do good,
I have sinned against you
whom I should love above all things.
I firmly intend, with your help,
to do penance,
to sin no more,
and to avoid whatever leads me to sin.
Our Savior Jesus Christ
suffered and died for us.
In his name, my God, have mercy.

Prayer for My Vocation

Dear God,
You have a great and loving plan
for our world and for me.
I wish to share in that plan fully,
faithfully, and joyfully.

Help me to understand what it is
you wish me to do with my life.
Help me to be attentive to the signs
that you give me about preparing for the future.

And once I have heard and understood
your call, give me the strength
and the grace to follow it
with generosity and love.

The Angelus

The angel of the Lord declared to Mary
and she conceived by the Holy Spirit.
Hail Mary....

Behold the handmaid of the Lord,
be it done to me according to your word.
Hail Mary....

And the Word was made Flesh
and dwelled among us.
Hail Mary....

Pray for us, O Holy Mother of God,
That we may be worthy of the promises of
Christ.

Let us pray:
Pour forth, we beseech you, O Lord,
your grace into our hearts
that we to whom the incarnation of
Christ your Son was made known by the
message of an angel may,
by his passion and cross,
be brought to the glory of his
resurrection, through Christ Our Lord. Amen.

Hail, Holy Queen

Hail, Holy Queen, Mother of Mercy;
hail, our life, our sweetness,
and our hope! To you do we cry,
poor banished children of Eve;
to you do we send up our sighs,
mourning and weeping in this vale of tears.

Turn, then, most gracious advocate,
your eyes of mercy toward us;
and after this our exile, show unto us
the blessed fruit of your womb, Jesus,
O clement, O loving, O sweet Virgin Mary!

Prayer of Saint Francis

Lord, make me an instrument of your peace:
  where there is hatred, let me sow love;
  where there is injury, pardon;
  where there is doubt, faith;
  where there is despair, hope;
  where there is darkness, light;
  where there is sadness, joy.

O Divine Master, grant that I may not
  so much seek
  to be consoled
  as to console,
  to be understood as to understand,
  to be loved as to love.

For it is in giving that we receive,
  it is in pardoning that we are pardoned,
  and it is in dying that we are born
  to eternal life.

The Rosary

A rosary has a cross, followed by one large bead and three small ones. Then there is a circle with five "decades." Each decade consists of one large bead followed by ten smaller beads. Begin the rosary with the sign of the cross. Recite the Apostles' Creed. Then pray one Our Father, three Hail Marys, and one Glory to the Father.

To recite each decade, say one Our Father on the large bead and ten Hail Marys on the ten smaller beads. After each decade, pray the Glory to the Father. As you pray each decade, think of the appropriate Joyful, Sorrowful, or Glorious Mystery, or a special event in the life of Jesus and Mary. Pray the Hail, Holy Queen as the last prayer of the rosary.

The Five Joyful Mysteries

1. The annunciation
2. The visitation
3. The birth of Jesus
4. The presentation of Jesus in the Temple
5. The finding of Jesus in the Temple

The Five Sorrowful Mysteries

1. The agony in the garden
2. The scourging at the pillar
3. The crowning with thorns
4. The carrying of the cross
5. The crucifixion and death of Jesus

The Five Glorious Mysteries

1. The resurrection
2. The ascension
3. The Holy Spirit comes upon the apostles
4. The assumption of Mary into heaven
5. The coronation of Mary in heaven

The Stations of the Cross

1. Jesus is condemned to die.
2. Jesus takes up His cross.
3. Jesus falls the first time.
4. Jesus meets His Mother.
5. Simon helps Jesus carry His cross.
6. Veronica wipes the face of Jesus.
7. Jesus falls the second time.
8. Jesus meets the women of Jerusalem.
9. Jesus falls the third time.
10. Jesus is stripped of His garments.
11. Jesus is nailed to the cross.
12. Jesus dies on the cross.
13. Jesus is taken down from the cross.
14. Jesus is laid in the tomb.

Holy Water

A holy water font containing blessed water is placed near the door of the church. When we enter the church, we put our fingers into the holy water and then make the sign of the cross. This action reminds us of the saving cross of Christ and the water of Baptism.

Blessing and Giving of Ashes

Ash Wednesday is the first day of Lent. On this day the Church uses the ashes of palms left over from Palm Sunday of the year before. The ashes of the palms are blessed and placed on our forehead in the sign of the cross. Ashes are an ancient sign of sorrow for sin and repentance and a reminder of death. Christians begin the Lenten season of penance by receiving them.

Blessing and Giving of Palms

The Sunday before Holy Week is called Passion Sunday or Palm Sunday. On Palm Sunday we remember the day on which Jesus Christ rode into Jerusalem and was greeted by the people with great joy. They welcomed Him as the Son of David, the Messiah, and broke off palm branches from the trees and waved them in the air. On this day, the Church blesses palms and gives them out to the people, who hold them during the reading of the Gospel. Many Christians bring the palms home and keep them as a remembrance of the saving work of Jesus.

Visits to the Blessed Sacrament

Catholics believe that Jesus Christ is truly present in our churches in the Blessed Sacrament. The Eucharist is kept in a tabernacle as Communion for the sick and for adoration. We *genuflect* (touch one knee to the floor) before going into the pew if the tabernacle is before us. We do not genuflect if the Blessed Sacrament is at a side chapel; we only bow to the altar. Genuflecting is a sign of our reverence for the presence of Jesus. Catholics go into church at other times besides the celebration of Mass and the sacraments to make a "visit," to take a few minutes to tell Jesus about our love, our needs, our hopes, our thanks.

Benediction of the Blessed Sacrament

Benediction is an ancient practice in the Church. The word *benediction* comes from the Latin word for "blessing." At Benediction a large Host, which was consecrated during Mass, is placed in a special holder called a "monstrance" so that all can see the Blessed Sacrament. The priest burns incense before the Blessed Sacrament. The incense is a sign of the adoration we offer in God's presence. The priest then lifts the monstrance and blesses the people by making a sign of the cross.

Glossary

apostles   A word meaning "those sent on a mission." It usually refers to the twelve special followers Jesus chose from among His disciples.

apostolic   A mark of the Church that identifies it as founded on Christ with Peter and the apostles as its first leaders and teachers. Their authority has been handed down to the Pope and bishops, their successors.

Blessed Trinity   The term used to signify that in God there are three divine persons: the Father, the Son, and the Holy Spirit. While we believe that there are three divine Persons who are distinct and equal, there is only one God.

catholic   The mark of the Church that identifies the Church as present all over the world with a message for all people. The Church welcomes people of every race and nationality. It is a universal, worldwide family of faith.

Christ   Jesus, the Messiah, God's Anointed One.

conscience   The ability we have to decide whether a thought, word, or deed is right or wrong.

disciples   The name given to all who follow Jesus Christ.

ecumenical council   A gathering of all the bishops of the world who, together with the Pope, discuss and make decisions concerning faith, morality, worship, and the entire life of the Church.

evangelization   Sharing the Good News of Jesus Christ with others and calling them to be disciples.

examination of conscience   An honest questioning of ourselves about our relationship with God and others. This can be done at anytime; it is essential to do it before celebrating the sacrament of Reconciliation.

faith   The virtue that enables us to believe in all God teaches and reveals to us, and to live according to the divine will.

Gospel   The word means "good news." It refers to the good news of salvation proclaimed first by Jesus and later by the apostles and the Church. The Gospel is interpreted and recorded in the Gospels of the four evangelists Matthew, Mark, Luke, and John.

grace   God's free gift to us of a share in the divine life.

heaven   The state of everlasting happiness with God.

hell   The state of final separation from God due to our deliberate choice of sin.

holiness   A mark of the Church that identifies it as a people called to live in loving relationship with God, who alone is holy, and one another through prayer, the sacraments, and service.

hope   The virtue that helps us to trust in God's promise that evil will never overcome good.

Immaculate Conception   The belief Catholics share that Mary was free from original sin from the first moment of her life because she was to be the mother of Christ.

Kingdom of God   The term used by Jesus to describe the power of God's love active in our world and the world to come.

Law of Love   Love the Lord your God with all your heart, with all your soul, with all your strength, and with all your mind. Love your neighbor as you love yourself.

liturgy The official public worship of the Church as distinguished from private devotion.

love The greatest of all virtues. It draws us into a relationship of intimacy with God and expresses itself in generosity, forgiveness, and sacrifice for others.

Mass The Lord's Supper; the celebration of the Eucharist; the Church's great prayer of praise and thanksgiving.

mortal sin The deliberate choice to break off our whole relationship with God. For a sin to be mortal it must do serious harm to our relationship with God, others, or self; it must be done with full and clear knowledge of its seriousness; it must be done freely and with full intent.

New Testament The second part of the Bible, consisting of twenty-seven books about Jesus Christ, His message, His mission, and His first followers.

Old Testament The first part of the Bible, consisting of forty-six books that express the faith of the Israelite people, the ancient Jews and our ancestors in faith.

oneness A special mark of the Church that identifies its unity of faith, discipline, and structure.

original sin The first sin of humanity; the sin of Adam and Eve that affects all human beings.

paschal mystery A term that designates the most important aspects of our redemption: Christ's death, resurrection, and ascension.

Passover A feast in which the Jews celebrate the deliverance of their ancestors from slavery in Egypt.

Pentecost The name given to the day on which the Holy Spirit came upon the disciples. It comes fifty days after Easter.

prayer Talking and listening to God. Prayer can be private or communal.

purgatory A process of purification after death if a person has sinned.

resurrection The mystery through which God raised Jesus Christ from the dead.

sacraments Effective signs of God's presence among us; seven special signs that effect, or bring about, what they signify. The seven sacraments are: Baptism, Confirmation, Eucharist, Penace or Reconciliation, Anointing of the Sick, Matrimony, and Holy Orders.

Sacraments of Initiation The three sacraments by which we become fully initiated members of the Church: Baptism, Confirmation, and Eucharist.

Scriptures The written word of God; another name for the Bible.

sin Freely choosing to do what we know is wrong; disobeying God's law on purpose.

social sin Sins we commit as a society, as a group. Some examples are racism, sexism, religious hatred.

temptation An attraction to sin; it is not a sin.

tradition The word literally means "handed on." In our Church it refers to the truths, beliefs, and practices that have come to us from the time of Jesus and the apostles.

transubstantiation A term used to describe the sacramental mystery by which the bread and wine become the Body and Blood of Christ while retaining the appearance of bread and wine.

venial sin A sin that is less serious than mortal sin. It does not break completely our relationship with God. It does weaken it.

virtue A habit of doing good.

Index

Index